PASTORAL CARE AS DIALOGUE

Joachim Scharfenberg

PASTORAL CARE AS DIALOGUE

Translated by O. C. Dean, Jr.

FORTRESS PRESS PHILADELPHIA

Translated by O. C. Dean, Jr.

Translated from the German *Seelsorge als Gespräch,* 3d edition,

Library of Congress Cataloging-in-Publication Data

Scharfenberg, Joachim, 1927–
Pastoral care as dialogue.

Translation of: Seelsorge als Gespräch. 3rd ed.
1. Pastoral counseling. 2. Dialogue—Religious aspects—Christianity. I. Title.
BV4012.2.S313 1987 253.5 86–45921
ISBN 0–8006–1958–7

2101J86 Printed in the United States of America 1-1958

Contents

Translator's Preface

Dialogue is the heart of pastoral care and counseling. This statement may be so self-evident that we take it for granted and fail to realize the many ways in which dialogue itself, by its very nature, helps to accomplish the goals of counseling: to free a person from unconscious enslavement to the past, to help that person find his or her real self, and to exercise that new freedom and new self. We may also overlook the fact that some pastors consider the counseling situation a good opportunity to seek other goals, such as proclaiming the gospel, promulgating God's law, and evoking repentance and confession.

In this volume, Joachim Scharfenberg seeks to correct these and other oversights and misconceptions. More than this, he provides a theoretical and theological foundation as well as practical guidelines for the operation of dialogue within the context of pastoral care and counseling.

American readers will find that the first part of chapter 1 relates specifically to the situation in German Protestant pastoral care and to that extent is mainly of academic interest, but the author moves quickly in the remainder of the chapter to apply linguistic theory to his examination of dialogue. Chapter 2 discusses how pastoral dialogue draws on and goes beyond various other types of dialogue, and chapter 3 applies some important insights of psychotherapy to the pastoral-counseling situation. The three remaining chapters provide detailed practical guidance on means and methods, problems and procedures in counseling. Case studies are used throughout to make the discussion more concrete.

In regard to the translation, there are just two comments. In the German-speaking world, the use of masculine pronouns as common gender, referring to both male and female, is still quite well accepted. I have not attempted to change this practice and use inclusive pronouns, since to do so not only would be unfaithful to the original but would also have enormously complicated the task of translation. Terms such as "man" and "mankind," however, have been avoided, and the use of exclusive pronouns has intentionally been kept to a minimum.

The German word *Gespräch,* usually translated here as "dialogue," also means "discussion" or "conversation," and these terms have occasionally been used. Etymologically, however, "dialogue" is particularly appropriate to Scharfenberg's view of pastoral care, for its root meaning in Greek conveys the idea of "talking through" one's problems and difficulties. The goal of that talking-through, in the author's view, is to help the counselee find new freedom and new possibilities for creative living. Theologically, the aim is not just to proclaim God's Word but in and through the counseling process to help the dialogue partner apply its liberating power to his or her life.

O. C. DEAN, JR.

Preface

Practical theology, particularly the teaching of pastoral care, has awakened from what just a few years ago was still deplored as its "Sleeping Beauty slumber" (Rudolf Bohren). Whether the role of the one who "kissed it awake" is to be ascribed to the scientific study of human behavior or to the steadily growing trend toward clinical pastoral education can only be decided finally by historians of a later time. The work offered here is, in any case, completely shaped by this dynamic process. Not originally intended for publication, it was conceived in large part several years ago and presented in lectures at the universities of Tübingen and Kiel. The fact that students and pastors have duplicated the material on their own and obviously found it helpful in preparation for their professional tasks has encouraged me to have it published.

It was not possible throughout to maintain the intended basic character of a textbook imparting confirmed results that transcend discussions of current theological issues. Occasionally critical-polemical inquiry dominates. The abundance of different viewpoints, which at first glance could perhaps be a little confusing, should be understood as a kind of inoculation against the understandable desire for ready-made prescriptions. Although I have tried to bring the manuscript up to date with the latest discussions in the field, some authors cited may feel themselves wedded to positions they no longer hold today. Also, important recent publications could not be considered. A basic concern of mine, however, has been to delineate clearly and discuss thoroughly once again one of the most important advances of our day, namely, the movement beyond the concept of pastoral care as pure proclamation.

Kiel, March 1972 JOACHIM SCHARFENBERG

Preface to the American Edition

It is with mixed emotions that I present to the English-speaking public this textbook written more than a decade and a half ago.

On the one hand, my thinking has changed and expanded during the intervening time. Today I would try to say more clearly and precisely much of what I could only suggest in this book. At this point I would at least like to mention briefly the points at which the present work now seems in need of expansion.

1. The polemic against Eduard Thurneysen can only be understood historically and is explained by the decades-long dominance of dialectical theology in Germany; here and there it will strike the American reader as strange. Since then I have sought, in ever-new approaches, to do better justice to Thurneysen's legitimate concerns, which had—above all in the Nazi period—a significance for German practical theology that cannot be overestimated.

2. The significance of transference for pastoral care is merely stated in this book; no stimulus toward a specifically pastoral treatment of it is offered. At this point Heinz Kohut's more recent studies in self-psychology have opened up the possibility of recognizing and dealing intentionally with a specifically religious transference.

3. I would like very much to maintain my view of language as the point of convergence between psychoanalysis and pastoral care. Today, however, it appears to me to be a specific kind of linguistic behavior, namely symbolic communication, that I would commend to the particular attention of pastors. Along with Paul Tillich, I am now deeply convinced that a more profound understanding of symbolism offers the key both

to the depths of the human soul and to the little-used treasures of the Christian tradition, with which pastors ought to be familiar.

In order to give appropriate consideration to the points named above, a completely new book would have to be written. Therefore, I can only refer to publications that have appeared in the meantime, especially my *Einführung in die Pastoralpsychologie* (Introduction to pastoral psychology; Göttingen, 1985), which one can hope will also appear in English one day!

On the other hand, naturally, I rejoice that through this translation my thinking is a little more accessible to my many English-speaking friends. Toward that end, of course, a substantial contribution has been made by the fresh and lively translation of Dr. O. C. Dean, Jr., and at this point I would like to offer him my heartfelt thanks for his dedicated and sensitive work. May this book serve also in the English-speaking world as a helpful orientation for beginning pastors!

Kiel, October 1986 JOACHIM SCHARFENBERG

Introduction

Nowhere has the separation of theory and practice in German Protestant theology had more disastrous consequences than in the field of pastoral care. It expressed itself in the fact that decade after decade nice-sounding theological prescriptions were formulated for what was supposed to take place in pastoral care and theoretical treatises were written on a subject for which, however, there was no corresponding practical application. On the other hand, the practitioner, who saw himself left in the lurch by the textbooks, had to turn his lack of theory into method and, in an almost irresponsible way, dabble around in the tasks he found confronting him in actual practice. Also, insight into this state of affairs was even to a large extent obstructed by especially stubborn efforts to prevent the introduction of empirical methods of research into the realm of pastoral care. Even today the application of empirical methods of investigation in this area is felt by many to be something of a sacrilege. The secrecy of confession and the pastoral duty of silence might be violated, it is said, if one opens the confidentiality of pastoral counseling to case discussions and dialogue analyses; and the "success" of pastoral dialogue is, in any case, not an empirically ascertainable quantity but a "seed of hope," an incidental gift of the Spirit, who blows where he will.

In contrast to this, nevertheless, one must point out that the reliability of the psychoanalytical method, both within the discipline and in the view of the general public, has in no way suffered from being open from the beginning to methodological verification and scientific discussion within the circle of responsibly thoughtful and discreet colleagues. The suspicion arises that the theological argument is used as a welcome pretext to spare oneself the wholesome shock of what, in actual ecclesiastical practice, is desired on the part of church members and what is offered by members of the clergy under the heading of pastoral care.[1] Only the fact that pastoral care today is threatened with the complete loss of its monopoly and sees itself exposed to secular competition of various kinds and shapes seems to be leading gradually to a change here that is beginning to make itself evident above all in the discussion of foreign literature on the topic.[2]

Nonetheless, it is not enough for the practice of pastoral care to be opened up—under outside pressure, as it were—to empirical methods of research. These would presumably remain ineffectual if the critique did not penetrate to the core of theological reflection itself, which still largely undergirds our theories of pastoral care. It is a thesis of this book that the rigid bonding of the two concepts "dialogue" and "proclamation"—whereby the latter is still based on a "linguistic concept with higher ordination"[3]—has, to a great extent, hindered the practical application of the theory of pastoral care. This unhappy connection, which has penetrated deep into the consciousness of several generations of pastors, has also led to a persistent and striking disdain on the part of authors in practical theology for the theological method of correlation proposed by Paul Tillich.[4] Constrained by the idea that the accomplishment of proclamation is the goal of pastoral care, dialogue serves only as the starting point, prelude, or pretext for proclamation, so that the one who enters pastoral care is never put in a position to articulate the "question" he represents with his existence and thereby to make himself conscious of it.[5] Thus, for the most part, the pastor has answers ready for questions that are not even raised: theory and practice go their separate ways.

What if, nonetheless, we take seriously the linguistic structure of dialogue itself and attempt to appropriate what scholarly efforts in regard to this special structure have accomplished in the past and what has been learned recently through methodical, empirical investigation? Perhaps it could turn out that within this special structure of the dialogue—until now held in such low esteem—lies hidden what can be designated specifically as pastoral care, because dialogue can make one free and at the same time allow one to exercise this freedom.

The often-posed question of the *proprium* (proper place) of Protestant pastoral care should thus be viewed from a new angle. If the predominant interest of theology until now has been clearly to differentiate pastoral care from secular counseling techniques, in order thereby to leave its "proper" sphere untouched, then in this book exactly the opposite is to take place. By demonstrating the parallel between ways of thinking in the so-called secular sphere and certain theological methods, a possible identification of theological content in the theory and practice of secular forms of counseling should become feasible. The energetic concentration on the proper sphere of pastoral care and the nearly hermetic barrier between theology and the nontheological disciplines has, for an inordinately long time, guaranteed the theologian and professional cleric an identity that we find today increasingly questionable. The identity crisis in the ministerial profession—which is, in my opinion, rather belated and therefore often perceived only with horror—compels a rapprochement with nontheological efforts in behalf of humanity. These present themselves today in what has already become an almost boundless pluralism of method. The old theological task, to "test the spirits" and "hold fast what is good" (1 John 4:1; 1 Thess. 5:21), presents itself with new urgency. It no longer allows itself to be completed on the level of naively adopting a few psychological tricks and techniques but rather requires a careful discussion of the theological implications of the underlying theories—especially in the field of counseling. The following thoughts are intended to help sensitize one to this theoretical inquiry and at the same time provide practical help.

1. Pastoral Care and Language

THESIS: A great many ideas about dialogue within the new literature on pastoral care must be regarded as leading to misconceived forms of dialogue, because they entice one into an authoritarian or methodical misuse of language and easily draw one under the influence of clerical tendencies toward self-assertion. Verbal interchange between two or more persons means forgoing exactness in the mathematical sense, objectivity in the epistemological sense, and information in the authoritarian sense. Through its basic circular structure, dialogue can hand a person his freedom and place at his disposal an opportunity to practice this freedom. With the introduction of language as a means of therapy, depth psychology—similar in this regard to discerning pastors—has created in the dialogue a paradigm for nonauthoritarian interpersonal relations.

The near-tragic aspect of our situation consists in the fact that although there has never been so great a readiness for dialogue as there is today, the outcome of dialogue has repeatedly been failure. In all human relations there is almost a compulsion to talk. Since the individual is becoming ever more conscious of dependence on others, creative work is achieved largely through the cooperative activity of several people, and that means through dialogue. People push themselves openly into conversation with others whom they believe to be better informed or more expert in certain areas of life.

No sooner have we entered the dialogical age, however, than

dialogue itself, its realization, and its completion have, to an increasing degree, become problematic and questionable. We are gradually beginning to suspect that dialogue is apparently not a life process that takes care of itself and can be taken for granted. Everything points toward one question. Dialogue is indeed important, but how does one do dialogue? It cannot be denied: we have all repeatedly experienced great distress and difficulty with dialogue. We participate in a conversation, but we are not understood. It seems to be a characteristic of discussions between scientists that in every third sentence the comment is made that someone has been misunderstood. We engage in dialogue, but we talk past one another. One gets the impression that our means of communication are inadequate for the purposes for which they are actually used. We speak on two levels, as it were. We form an image of the other person, yet our own speech does not affect him. Two partners stand opposite each other as if with closed visors. In this way they can carry on a conversation without having it lead to a real meeting. They are so devoted to the subject that nothing personal gets into the discussion, and the participants separate, feeling a certain fruitlessness and sterility. On the other hand, it can happen that we carry on a conversation and get the impression that the sole purpose of this conversation is for someone to get something off his chest. The speaker's own emotional state pushes itself so disturbingly to the forefront that there can be no real communication, no genuine sharing. Or a discussion takes place, and we get the feeling that it is not being taken seriously. Everyone remains noncommittal, so that very often what is left at the end of the conversation is only rumor and idle talk. Something falls apart during the discussion, and we have the feeling that the pieces cannot be got together again.

Dialogue itself seems to be sick, and there are radical critics who have placed a heavy burden of blame on dialogue itself. Through dialogue, as it is widely carried on today, a human being can—in the opinion of Joachim Bodamer—"be transformed into a spiritual machine that must have as little mystery about it as possible. The person is degraded, demystified, and thereby robbed of his personal inner substance, his silent substance, and destroyed in his essence."[1] The same writer makes fun of the view "that we get closer to a phenomenon, perhaps indeed experience ourselves again and can live on that, if we form it into words, describe it, get it in our sights, conjure it up with speech."[2] So often today one encounters the prejudice that for the needs of our day, consciousness, explanation, and understanding still in no way mean healing and redemption; but hidden behind this idea, it seems to me, is precisely the attitude that starts from a fatefully erroneous assessment of language and can lead only to a misuse—and thus to various misconceived forms—of dialogue.

THE MISUSE OF DIALOGUE IN PROTESTANT PASTORAL CARE

In the realm of Protestant pastoral care this erroneous assessment of language expresses itself in the ever-persistent conviction that dialogue—if it is to qualify as pastoral dialogue—must always involve proclamation. This conviction was first formulated by Hans Asmussen with his definition that pastoral care is dialogue "from man to man in which the individual is told the gospel straight to his face."[3]

Dialogue instructions that are based on Asmussen's concept of pastoral care are intended not to give a person freedom but rather to take him prisoner. Since the mesh of the net with which the sermon tries to catch people is too coarse, a finer-meshed net is needed in order to catch a person, and that net is dialogue. Dialogue is chosen for that sole purpose, and therefore the church member must speak, so that he can offer places to attack and thus be trapped in his own words. Actually the dialogue partner finds himself in the role of hearer, but he must also speak, so that he can betray himself. In this way, the upper hand in such a dialogue is determined from the beginning: it belongs to the pastor. Through it he is in command, with "dignity and tact." Asmussen demands that the dignity of appearance of the leader of such a dialogue correspond to the loftiness of his claim, namely, to appear and to speak in the name of God. Thus the dialogical character, the reciprocity between pastor and hearer, is something completely preliminary, something to be overcome, in which the hearer has only to betray himself, to offer points of attack, so that in these weak places the proclamation can be brought to bear in such a way that it will stick, will strike home, and the one struck will be seized, captured, imprisoned. Proclamation can never be discussion; it is rather the end of discussion.[4]

For Eduard Thurneysen as well, proclamation is the central point toward which dialogue must be directed. The model concept after which dialogue must be patterned is what Thurneysen calls liturgical dialogue.[5] This is the dialogue that God leads and into which God draws a human being so that the person's response is, in return, directed toward God. It is a matter of praise and prayer. But such use of language, evoked by God and responding to God, is called liturgy. The response that a human being can make vis-à-vis God is always a liturgical one, "that is to say, a response that stands in service to the word of God." Thurneysen claims that pastoral dialogue is to be understood as a special form of this liturgical dialogue. It is distinguished from every other dialogue by the primacy of the "Word and Spirit of God." Therefore the aim of every pastoral dialogue can only be that it gradually change, even in the literal sense, into liturgical dialogue, that in it the Word of God be read and interpreted, that there be prayer and praise to God. Only when a dialogue between two people has been successfully placed under the power of the Word of God—only then has a pastoral dialogue taken place. It is essential "that the Word of God descend into every human spiritual ferment." The pastor who conducts such a dialogue can thus never give way to the style of a real dialogue but must always have in mind how to transform it into just such a liturgical dialogue. Characteristic, at this point, are the images that Thurneysen employs: the pastor must feel as if he has been sent on patrol; he may not let himself be cut off from home base, for "God must come into his own with his Word in all areas of human life."[6]

How this works out in practice can also be studied in the occasional examples that Thurneysen gives. He describes a wife who comes to the pastor because she suffers from unbearable headaches that are related to her inability to experience sexual satisfaction in marriage. That much has already been determined by a psychiatrist. Thurneysen sees the task of the pastoral dialogue as, if possible, not going into this need at all. Rather, the woman in question "must receive light and truth from God's Word, her sins must be uncovered and her forgiveness made known, so that in the light of this forgiveness she can begin a new life."[7] Yet how the dialogue partner can be won over to such a purpose and how there can ever be real participation by the partner in such a dialogue—on these things, curiously, Thurneysen does not reflect at all. He himself feels that technical advice that goes into detail for counseling of this sort is extraordinarily difficult. Therefore one finds very little of it in Thurneysen's teachings on pastoral care. He returns, rather, to the primacy of the Holy Spirit and constantly emphasizes that on the part of the pastor, "listening must first and simultaneously become obedience to God's Word, which teaches us to understand humanity and human things in general."[8] Hence it can come as no surprise at all that the one destination toward which everything in Thurneysen is steered again and again is the advice to pray.[9] Thus pastoral care is fulfilled only when the concrete human need—which someone faces without orientation, understanding, or strength—is transcended, as it were, and liturgical dialogue with God takes place. That this can be really possible in only an infinitesimally small number of pastoral dialogues is apparently never considered.

It would be a mistake if one were to assume that the two classical figures in German Protestant pastoral care, Asmussen and Thurneysen, and their basic positions, have been overcome today. Until a few years ago, almost all the books that appeared in West Germany on the topic of Protestant pastoral care held to the idea that in pastoral care proclamation must occur and that therefore the control of the dialogue demanded by Asmussen and Thurneysen cannot be given up.

The main theme of the newer teachings in pastoral care—in total disregard of changes in sociological structure—is that of the spiritual father. In beautiful naiveté, the dialogue partner is designated the "pastoral child," and the pastor is given the task of judging, as father and mother do.[10]

Thus the object of counseling, understood in this way, must be to lead the dialogue to a "break." The dialogue is characterized by a dividing line and operates, therefore, on two levels:[11]

> However softly and smoothly the dialogue begins, it will at some point experience a break initiated by the pastor. Then it will receive a new beginning, which the pastor will determine. The pastor will prefer to terminate the discussion rather than give up control of the dialogue, because he comes not as a private individual but as the bearer of an office. When I relinquish the leadership of a dialogue, I become unfaithful to my Lord.[12]

The thesis of a break within the pastoral dialogue is not a specifically new discovery in the proclamation-oriented teachings on pastoral care of Asmussen and Thurneysen. It is also to be found in the more psychologically defined pastoral-care teachings that seek to orient themselves toward medical practice. The thesis of the break is most clearly and instructively expressed by Horst Fichtner, who, along with other authors, has worked it out in an explicit methodology of the dialogue. The following directions are given. First, the pastor is supposed to ask the "foster child" certain questions defined by examples out of the pastor's own life and then proceed in the following manner:

> After the stream of speech has begun to flow, the pastor must carefully watch for an opportunity to present itself that will allow him unnoticed to turn the dialogue away from personal questions and toward the purely pastoral. This opportunity must be sought and found so that the dialogue can end with a heart-reaching, conscience-awakening appeal that is directed toward the understanding of the foster child and moves him, with words of some appropriate Scripture passage, into the light of responsibility before God. The dialogue may be divided into a more worldly and a more pastoral part. . . . The pastor must see to it that the worldly part becomes shorter and shorter. Then, after a still deeper level has been reached, one points to the grace of God and, by activating the power of the will, restrains the primary effective motives or suppresses in the foster child the stirrings of worldly conditioned desires.[13]

Such directions for pastoral care thus consider the personal problems of the one coming into pastoral care as something completely irrelevant that must be pushed aside as quickly as possible. The real goal must be reached—and that is, with the help of suitable words of Scripture, to bring about a suppression of desire. We are dealing here with the kind of pastoral-care practice that led the Berlin physician Eberhard Schaetzing to speak of so-called ecclesiogenic neuroses.

What is deeply disappointing, however, is that until recently not even the newer influences on pastoral dialogue, which are more oriented toward depth psychology, have been able to free themselves from this rigidity of method. Thus even, for example, with Adolf Allwohn, the one entering pastoral care appears as the object of particular psychotechnical manipulations. He writes, "The most important thing is to awaken a consciousness of guilt and a longing for redemption. The person is supposed to appear as helpless, yearning, and tormented."[14] And for a long time even Hans-Joachim Thilo could not free himself from this understanding of the so-called pastoral child and his opposite in a conflict situation: "The pastor must know that the person placing himself into dialogue can absolutely do nothing else but hide himself from what the pastor has to say or to ask. Now, it is the task of the pastor to bring his pastoral child to the point where he is willing, on his own, more and more to put his mask aside."[15] Even here psychological technique is used only to develop a good psychological method of interrogation "in order to push forward to the actual, hidden state of misconduct, indeed, of sin and guilt."[16]

Even Adelheid Rensch's detailed introduction to pastoral dialogue[17] is unable to free itself from this way of thinking. Pastoral dialogue, in Rensch's view, is characterized by a radical closeness to the original dialogue: the dialogue between God and humanity. It must be invested with the claim of seeking the structure-defining middle—and thus the totality—of the person. Hence, pastoral dialogue can make use of all other forms of dialogue, but they are regarded only as transition stages to its real goal, and it must claim for itself the culmination of each and every special form of dialogue. In every case, proclamation must remain the goal, yet the case itself will determine when it occurs. Other forms of dialogue qualify as pastoral dialogue only when they also work toward the rebirth and salvation of the person. Therefore pastoral dialogue has to orient itself toward that unfortunate construction designated widely as the "pastoral care of Jesus"; that is, it requires a "method and manner that seek to come close to Christ's penetrating understanding of humanity."[18] After laying the foundation and setting the goal in this way, one cannot turn oneself over to the freedom of real dialogue; rather, this freedom must be restricted by methodological instructions. The dialogue moves through an initial phase into a diagnostic phase that must be followed by a phase of consultation and proclamation of the Word, which is presented as an aid to faith and crowned with a phase of practical help toward the realization of the knowledge of faith, designated as aids to faith and life.[19]

Let us attempt to summarize our critique. Any kind of counseling must be called authoritarian if its purpose is to use dialogue only to carry out some prescribed plan that is oriented toward the past, already known, and at one's disposal. The linguistic event is thus restricted here in an objectifying manner, just as it is wherever one tries to proceed according to a prescribed method that, in an unchangeable basic structure, seeks to accomplish the same result, even with strategically appropriate modifications in individual cases. The method is indeed "liturgical," for it seeks to ritualize the living flow of dialogue, to direct it onto a prescribed track. Thereby, however, pastoral care acquires the character of a religious "celebration" that, in a kind of compulsive repetition, lets one reach the same eternal orbit around the same center point. The resulting sociological and psychological problems can be made especially clear in the example of individual confession.

THE PROBLEM OF CONFESSION AND DIALOGUE

Beyond the two classical views of pastoral care by Asmussen and Thurneysen, the newer teachings in the field, to the extent that they are oriented toward proclamation as the central task of pastoral dialogue, also have confession in view as the actual goal of dialogue. Thus Thilo writes that in most cases pastoral dialogue will be the necessary preparation for confession.[20] Allwohn asserts that the "inner tendency toward confession" must dwell within every pastoral dialogue.[21] This clear trend toward a regeneration of Protestant confession seems to have received substantial support from the Evangelical church conferences (*Kirchentage*), where unusually strong pressure toward confession and individual dialogue has been observed. This has been interpreted in various quarters as a renaissance of individual confession blazing its own new trail within the Evangelical church.[22]

In contrast to this movement, we must emphasize as clearly as possible that one can hardly imagine a greater difference than that between dialogue and confession. According to the Protestant understanding, the office of confession can only be the service that one brother does for another when, responding to penitent confession and acting in Christ's stead, he grants forgiveness of sins. It can be used only where it is a question of consoling a frightened and troubled conscience, strengthening faith through an outward sign, and rebuilding the shattered communion with God and neighbor. Thus it was a particular situation that the Reformers had in mind when they placed a high value on confession even within the Protestant church: the situation of a person suffering from an impugned and troubled conscience. The question now is whether this psychological situation might still exist today as a mass phenomenon. Perhaps a few sociological considerations will prove helpful here.

In his book *The Lonely Crowd*, sociologist David Riesman attempted a correlation between types of character and forms of society, which became extraordinarily well known and accepted. In it the tradition-directed, inner-directed, and other-directed types of people are each related to particular social situations.[23]

The world of the tradition-directed person offers a hierarchy of eternal values perceived in an external order and guaranteed by authorities, institutions, and traditions; and the individual needs only to find his place in that order. Guilt in this society is experienced primarily as a fall from the eternal order. The classical form of pastoral care in this world is therefore the Roman Catholic institution of confession, which guarantees to the person with a strong and sensitive conscience a contented existence through reconciliation with the institution and the imposition of a penance.

In the world of the inner-directed person, guidance and ethical orientation come more strongly from within. The category of the individual is discovered. A high value is placed on personality, and conscience is given a significance it did not have in earlier epochs. The reformulation of pastoral care in the intellectual and awakening emotional sense corresponds to this inward shift in orientation.

Now, in our time people seem to be especially oriented toward others: they are "other-directed." The prerequisite for a strong internalization of norms of conscience no longer exists, because the individual no longer has available strong personalities with whom to identify and a unified, ordered system of commandments and prohibitions is no longer present. Guilt is therefore experienced neither primarily as a fall from an eternal order nor as a tormenting conflict of conscience; it manifests itself, rather, in a certain lack of orientation in the communal life of humanity. The classical question of the Reformation, "How do I find a God of grace?" seems to recede more and more into the background in the practice of pastoral care. Fewer and fewer people come to the pastor with an impugned and troubled conscience in order to be granted the forgiveness of sins. Even the development in the *Kirchentage* has shown that the longing for individual confession has declined in comparison with the urge for personal counseling or a pastoral dialogue in which the individual, together with another person, can talk through, better understand, and overcome his conflict situation.

In view of the completely changed psychic situation of humanity in our day, it thus seems that the psychological situation that led to the high value of confession no longer prevails. It can also be expected to have even less significance in the future.

The constantly raised demand that the goal of every pastoral dialogue be the confessional dialogue can therefore be labeled as only a romantic, lofty claim without any real content. Even regarded purely statistically, explicit confession plays only a small, dwindling role in today's pastoral care. Wherever one seeks to introduce it again, a serious question must be raised whether there are not underlying clerical inclinations that are concerned not so much with the suffering person and his or her difficulties as with the reduced social prestige of ecclesiastical office, which is thereby to receive a higher valuation of its authority. Even where confession is praised as therapy, a gross misunderstanding seems to prevail. The therapeutic effect of language lies not at all in the expression of conscious shortcomings but rather in the verbal reconstruction of traumatic scenes that have become unconscious and thus repressed.[24] Therefore, when people come to the pastor on their own with a desire for confession, one must first very carefully determine whether or not there is an underlying pathological process against which the completion of confession and the granting of forgiveness will necessarily remain completely ineffective.

For this writer's own life and education it may have been decisively significant that he, as a young and recently qualified curate serving in a hospital chaplaincy, encountered a woman who expressed the wish to be allowed to come for individual confession. A time was agreed upon when the ritual of confession prescribed by the liturgy could be carried out. The woman confessed her strong feelings of guilt about a petty trespass lying a decade in the past, and with the laying on of the hand, the forgiveness of this sin was pronounced upon her "to her face, in the place of and by command of the Lord Jesus Christ." On the next day, however, she again asked for counseling, in which she admitted that the act of confession had not freed her at all from her tormenting guilt feelings and expressed doubt that the chaplain, because of his youth and insufficient experience, could exercise his office with the desired effectiveness. She reported that she had, indeed, already made the same attempt fourteen times with as many different pastors and with the same negative results.

The challenge that may lie in such an experience—which is insignificant in itself and can certainly be reported in similar form by every experienced pastor—has long been avoided by seeing pastoral care as appropriate for the mentally healthy but psychotherapy as the effective means for cases of mental illness such as the one just described. In this connection, however, it must be clearly stated that a neat division between what is considered mentally ill and mentally well has become increasingly difficult. There are already voices claiming that neurotics are justified in protesting—however helplessly—against social conditions that have become inhuman, and that the real problem children even for psychotherapists are the so-called normal people, the well adjusted,[25] so that in a disarranged society the deranged must actually be designated as normal.[26] Be that as it may, the challenging question remains: Why, in certain, increasingly numerous cases, does pastoral comforting prove ineffectual, while psychotherapeutic efforts, on the other hand, are efficacious? Why is psychotherapy able to help even those who could not be helped through methods of pastoral care?

It seems to me a disastrous misunderstanding of the development of the Christian gospel in history that pastoral care has felt itself obliged to be oriented toward direct conformity to the Word and deed of Jesus. If Christian pastoral care no longer experiences the same success as that reported for Jesus—namely, that sickness yields to any kind of therapeutic manipulation, and psychic liberation succeeds merely upon the word of forgiveness—then it must have lost something that it will have to regain or else wait in humility for its return.[27]

It could also be, however, that the experiential presuppositions for such procedures and their implementation have changed in the course of historical development. Sigmund Freud contributed some very profound reflections on the problems under discussion here. He asked himself, namely, what was it about the words of Jesus to the paralytic, "Your sins are forgiven" (Mark 2:5), that becomes understandable against the background of psychoanalytical experience; and he designated the process a "call for unlimited transference," which bestows upon one who can thus speak a sheer overwhelming authority that is legitimated neither by tradition nor by law. He expresses the absolutely qualitative distance to such a possibility with the words, "Suppose I were to say to a patient, 'I, Professor Sigmund Freud, forgive you your sins.' What humiliation in my case!"[28] But when he continues by saying, "In the former case, however, the principle applies that analysis is not satisfied with success by suggestion but examines the origin and justification of the transference," at this point the real concern of this part of the Jesus tradition can be appropriately considered. The proper sphere of Protestant pastoral care is not the continued promotion of success by suggestion through the call for unlimited transference. Rather, to follow Jesus means to call into question the origin and justification of the traditionally asserted willingness for transference: "You have heard that it was said of old, but I say to you." The pastor cannot spare himself the "humiliation" that unavoidably occurs if he understands himself as the "follower" of Jesus in the sense that he can copy Jesus' mighty deeds and powerful words and believes he can simply steer unlimited willingness for transference into the channel of often very subtle and hidden clerical claims of authority. He will, however, be able to consider himself Jesus' follower to the extent that he attempts radically to call into question tradition-shaped wishes and needs for transference.

If the American theologian Peter Homans sees as an urgent theological duty the overcoming of the conceptual system of the "transference-God," which for him is identical with the God-concept of theism in Tillich's sense,[29] then for us here it should be a question of the realization and concretization of this concern in pastoral care. The pastoral way that must be walked with a person consists not in exploiting the willingness for transference that is perhaps still occasionally present, but in the consistent attempt repeatedly to call this willingness into question and thereby to knock down the idols that may be attractive even to the people of today. This will be accomplished not in a ritualized act that lays claim to the highest authority but in the arduous attempt to accompany a person along the way over a period of time, which can actually have a liberating effect.

Where confession has actually been brought back to life in the present day, the prerequisite for it has been a strong and viable community for the individual to stand in, such as that experienced in communitarian forms of life within the church and in communes and residential communities outside the church. Within such a communion, confession can remain viable not, of course, in the form of secret confession but in the form of self-critical group discussion, in which the individual is ready to admit personal mistakes and prejudices and submit them to the community for discussion. It is possible at this point that an element of the early Christian practice of confession within the community could again come to life. Yet that kind of form tied to a fixed, secret discipline should not be confused with the often painfully exhibitionist methods of the Moral Rearmament movement, which led to public confessions of sin that were often extremely offensive. Men and women in our day are apparently looking not for the father confessor of an obsolete patriarchal structure but for the open and willing partner to a dialogue that will unlock their freedom for them and reveal in them new possibilities for conflict resolution.

Thus the theological stance that seeks to find the pastoral element in the real character of dialogue consists in the key word "freedom." We can cite with hearty agreement Otto Haendler's theological stance on pastoral dialogue; it very clearly states that the aim of pastoral dialogue is the freedom of a Christian person and that proper pastoral care must keep the counselee clearly conscious of the feeling that he is being led from freedom to freedom.[30] The quest for the freedom of the Christian person will thus be the critical sounding board with which we will examine in the following section some basic concepts of dialogue, as we ask the question to what extent the character of language as information can serve as the basis for pastoral dialogue.

LANGUAGE AND INFORMATION

Pastoral care, as we read in almost all the textbooks of recent times, is proclamation in the form of dialogue. This is an engaging formula that, even into the present day, has retained a sort of taboo character: no one has dared seriously to question it or to criticize it. At the same time, writers have noticed from the beginning the strong logical tension that persists between the two concepts "proclamation" and "dialogue." "Proclamation" means the exhortation of something solid, unchangeable, objectively asserted, which one previously did not know about and which is passed on from one to another or others in a necessarily authoritarian fashion. "Dialogue," however, in principle means openness, ambiguity, the bipolar, reciprocal give-and-take of human speech. Can these opposites ever be united?

Does the opposition between dialogue and proclamation perhaps go even deeper than one has been inclined to assume? Are the two concepts perhaps the respective expressions of different conceptual structures and states of consciousness? Does their irreconcilability perhaps have far-reaching historical roots?

Recently Klaus Heinrich has again undertaken the attempt—not new in itself—to see our Western tradition as characterized by two different states of mind that are still operative in the present and in "profane" thinking. The one he calls the "myth-of-origin" state of mind, which he sees at work from Parmenides down to Martin Heidegger and Carl Gustav Jung, and for which the decisive point is the "genealogizing connection" back to the "origin." Opposed to this is the similarly ancient tradition in which "the element of propheticism is present in our history even in the profane forms of the Enlightenment,"[31] the central catchword of which is not "origin" but "association," *Bund.* It would be worth investigating the extent to which the domination of proclamation thinking in pastoral care is an expression of a basic, myth-of-origin way of thinking that can never free itself from the authoritarian posture of its connection back to the origin, while the key word "dialogue" gives impulses toward partnership as expressed in the idea of association, impulses that renounce finality and singleness of meaning, and—setting ever-new goals—open up the future, freedom, and new possibilities for living and solving problems.

Indeed, one must even raise the question whether proclamation, in its endeavor to be objective in the epistemological sense—which brings this process very close to information—does not destroy the characteristic basic structure of linguistic communication itself. In this regard, it was Wilhelm von Humboldt above all who, in his linguistic theory, proposed norms that are still valid today. For him, the characteristic nature of language consists in the binding together of two opposing views, according to which language either is alien to the soul and independent of it or belongs to the soul and is dependent on it.[32] That is, language joins "the world together with human beings in ever-repeated acts," and they "can no more produce it themselves than they can simply receive it from others." Only language can transfer an idea into real objectivity "without thereby losing its subjectivity."[33]

Humboldt described the actually circular structure of language in the following way. "Language is precisely object and independent to the extent that it is subject and dependent. For it never has, even in written form, a fixed abode but must always be generated anew in thinking and consequently must become completely subject; this very act of generation, however, includes turning language likewise into object; in this way it experiences each time the total effect of the individual. . . . The subjectivity of humanity as a whole, however, again becomes in itself something objective." Only with and through language is it possible "for objective truth to come forth out of the total strength of subjective individuality."[34]

The place where the hermeneutical circle of language becomes concrete is in relations with fellow human beings, for "a person understands himself only by testing the understandability of his words as he tries them out on others." This process is constantly kept in operation by the "longing for completion through others," which Humboldt views as an instinctive given of human nature. "Nothing appeals to a person so much as a lack of familiarity in which one suspects a deeper hidden agreement." Thus each ventured attempt is followed by a new one; language "is constantly and at every moment something transitory . . . not a work (*ergon*) but an activity (*energeia*)."[35]

In clear opposition to the concept of language as pure information, Humboldt sees as the unity and "breath of life" in language precisely the fact that "there is always something unknown that remains in it." "No one thinks with a word what another thinks, and even the smallest difference sends forth vibrations—if one wants to compare language with the most movable of all substances—through the whole language. . . . All understanding is therefore at the same time always a misunderstanding." Every word adds to a concept "significantly from itself." Therefore, it does a great deal more than just communicate itself. "It prepares the soul to understand more easily even what has not yet been heard; it makes clear what was heard long ago but then understood only half way or not at all, in that the similarity to what is now heard suddenly illuminates with a power that has since grown keener; and it creates the urge and the ability to move quickly more and more out of hearing and into understanding." Speaking with another person is thus "only a mutual awakening of the capacity to hear."[36]

In contrast to this, in the view of present-day American linguists, the conception of language from Aristotle to Wilhelm Wundt presents itself as a unified epoch. It is designated the "linguistic theory of tradition" and defined by the idea that in this period language was understood more or less exclusively as an "instrument for passing on ideas and knowledge (information)."[37] This tendency of linguistic understanding, which contains a distinctly objectifying character, may have reached its high point and at the same time its end point in Ludwig Wittgenstein's conception of language in his *Tractatus Logico-Philosophicus*, written before and during World War I and published for the first time in 1921.[38] In it he brings to expression his basic conception that "the world is everything that is the case," which lets everything that is the case be determined by the totality of the facts coming together out of "circumstances." For him, accordingly, linguistic understanding means "knowing what is the case" when a sentence is true.[39] As Karl Otto Apel has shown, Wittgenstein thus stands completely within traditional linguistic theory, which strives toward the "logistic construction of a philosophical language of precision." He envisions a language of symbols that belongs "to logical grammar"; that is, "the outcome of philosophy is not philosophical statements but the clarification of statements." Since a statement can impart meaning, Wittgenstein can practically equate meaning with information content and thereby reduce the problem of understanding to the "logical interpretation of information about facts."[40]

With clear emotion, he turns against any psychological understanding, for "the thinking, conceptualizing subject does not exist. . . . The subject does not belong to the world; it is rather a boundary of the world."[41] He thereby identifies, in a radical transcendentalization, "the metaphysical subject as boundary of the world with the logical subject of language in general." Thus it comes to a distinction between what can be said and what cannot, which in its ramifications for philosophy results in the possibility not only of thinking in terms of true and false, but also of declaring most of the statements and questions of philosophy meaningless, and thus of directing a critique "against the claim to meaning of the text itself."[42] This gives expression to a suspicion of meaninglessness that has long ruled the positivistic sciences and that had disastrous consequences in psychiatry before Freud.

With this logical treatment of language—which Wittgenstein himself later abandoned—a road was taken that led to an ever-greater transformation of language into information, on the one hand, and which, on the other, must be termed objectifying in the strict sense of the word. Since there are apparently rather varied ideas of what objectification actually is, especially in present-day theology, I would like to use here a definition from Werner Heisenberg, which can lead to helpful clarity and to which I propose to hold in what follows. Heisenberg writes, "We objectify an assertion when we maintain that its content is not dependent on the conditions under which it can be verified."[43]

This definition indicates the point at which later development can no longer follow the initial steps of the early Wittgenstein. The impetus toward a rethinking comes quite substantially from modern physics. Thus the physicist and philosopher Carl Friedrich von Weizsäcker, in response to the question of whether language can be reduced to information in Wittgenstein's sense, is inclined to answer no.[44] A language that is brought up on its content of information becomes telegram style, which Weizsäcker calls the "parade march of a drill" and is only possible "against the backdrop of a language that is not transformed into unambiguous information."[45]

Above all, the concomitant pretensions to objectivity are rejected by modern natural scientists, and the assumption "that we can describe the world without speaking of ourselves"[46] is exposed as an illusion. Modern physics has thus upset positions that were adopted especially in the wake of the historicizing and psychologizing hermeneutic of the eighteenth and nineteenth centuries. To be sure, great thinkers of the last century, in anticipation of today's knowledge, were already questioning the idea of the objectifying function of language. Johann Gustav Droysen ascertained that what was taking place in language was actually the opposite of an objectification process: "In language the spirit subjectifies the world." Every process of understanding and interpretation adds something to the text that was not there before. So-called objectivity thus proves to be an illusion and also appears generally undesirable. Droysen could say, "I thank you for this emasculated kind of objectivity."[47]

The development of later linguistic theories has thus followed Humboldt rather than the early Wittgenstein, for the individual parts of Humboldt's views sketched above reappear in the work of modern linguists. With Klaas Heeroma we read that all texts of any significance contain "an element of hyperphasia" and that tradition and interpretation work together on a text and turn it into something different from what it was originally.[48] The greatest weight, however, must perhaps be given to Heisenberg's determination that in the new physics one must also give up the hope of constructing a purely informative language of precision. His concept of "probability function" unites objective and subjective elements, and it is observation that has a destabilizing effect on the probability function; for this reason, the quantum theory no longer allows a fully objective description of nature. Consequently, the ideal of objectivity, which had earlier been the basis of all the natural sciences, is also surrendered in this field. Heisenberg states finally "that the concept of complementarity, which was introduced into the explanation of the quantum theory by Niels Bohr, has encouraged physicists to use an equivocal rather than an unequivocal language."[49]

Thus the hopes for an ideal of absolute exactitude that would be derived from an eternal and universally identical human nature have not been fulfilled. On the contrary, "scientific thinking" has developed a host of different dialects or technical languages. In his later work, Wittgenstein takes this state of affairs into account in his *Philosophical Investigations* with the term "language game," *Sprachspiel.* For our discussion, two traits of this peculiar expression seem to be important:

1. With the term "game," *Spiel,* says Wittgenstein, "the scope of the concept is not limited by a boundary." "The concept 'game' is a concept with blurry edges"; but "is not lack of sharpness often just what we need?"[50] This changes the basic attitude toward language. An attitude that strives for information becomes an attitude in which hermeneutics predominates. That is, the language game raises investigation to a new level where "we do not want to learn something new with it. We want to understand something that already lies obvious before our eyes." Therefore the essence of language becomes "something that lies under the surface, . . . that lies within, . . . that is supposed to be dug out by an analysis." It is a question of discovering "depth," of a "deep grammar,"[51] of a struggle against the "bewitching of our understanding through the means of our language."[52] The means of such therapy[53] ("The philosopher treats the question like a sickness")[54] is as follows: "We lead words back again from their

metaphysical to their everyday application."[55] In this way the use of words is again interwoven with extralinguistic activity, and the term "language game" is supposed to emphasize that the speaking of language "is a part of an activity or a form of living."[56] Language games, as Apel expressed it, are "models of linguistic usage, of forms of living, and of opening up the world."[57]

2. There is, however, a second aspect of the term "language game": "The agreement that obtains in language and is supposed to make understanding possible is not an agreement in the nature of humankind or an agreement of opinions, but an agreement in the form of living."[58] Every understanding of meaning presupposes participation in the language game. This always means that language can be understandable only for the participants in a particular language game, of which there are innumerably many, and that understanding is interwoven with doing, with "activities." Wittgenstein handles the establishment of the rules of the game in a way that is loose and almost relativizing: for him there are even times when we play and make up the rules as we go along.[59] A rule is only a signpost, but following the rule is a practice that has to do with "customs";[60] and the common human way of behaving is the "system of reference by means of which we explain to ourselves a language."[61] In this sense one can also speak of hermeneutical language games in cases such as "the telling a story handed down or experienced, . . . the exposition of an old text, . . . a sermon, lecture, school lesson, etc."[62]

Understanding within such language games succeeds, however, not only because of a common human nature; it is also founded on relationship. "Understanding stops if the relationship comes to an end."[63] Benjamin Whorf introduced into linguistic understanding the concept of the "matrix of relations," and with his statement that "rapport constitutes the real essence of thought insofar as it is linguistic,"[64] he gave convincing expression to the relational reality of language and confirmed Jean-Paul Sartre's statement "The problem of language is parallel to that of love."[65] Thus we can also agree with Heeroma, who observed that the full truth of language is experienced by a person above all in the internal language of his thoughts but that there are always certain communities of trust and faith that give him guarantees for his faith: the family, his circle of friends, the church. Also, in these, language can function again and again as genuine truth.[66]

We may summarize this section of the chapter as follows: Modern linguists have developed a dualistic theory of language. In addition to the traditional linguistic theory based on information, there was "recognized a noncognitive kind of function and meaning of language, that is, one that is not dependent on any element of understanding and knowledge."[67] One does justice to this task by recognizing in science the limited nature of the various "language games" and by seeking their truth content in the language of poets. In particular, this means the following:

1. Werner Heisenberg has shown that in physics there is no longer a precise language in which one can use the normal logical process of deduction. The modern development has superseded the Aristotelian principle of contradiction with the motto "Tertium non datur." Between true and false there is a whole range of assertions that possess relative "truth value" (Weizsäcker). It is most important, however, to remind oneself again and again that each word or concept has only a limited area of application. But since we never know very exactly where the limits of its application lie, "it will never be possible through rational thinking alone to arrive at an absolute truth."[68] Thus an insistence on the requirement of a complete and logical clarity would make science impossible.

2. To the extent that an unambiguous logical truth becomes impossible for science, interest has shifted to the truth content of the poetic word. It has already been sought by the aforementioned linguist Heeroma. He shows that "language can no longer be true for science and science no longer for language."[69] In science, accuracy has taken the place of truth, while the poet says something that is true only in language. He

gives intimations that cannot stand the test of critical reflection. Why does he do that? Because the poetic word does not intend to pass on information; it intends, rather, to evoke associations. So the criterion of truth lies not in "objective circumstances"; credibility and incredibility come from listening alone. "A person experiences his truth and his falsehood in language; a person experiences his language in the ear."[70] Thus it is up to the listening ear whether language is true, whether it is right, whether one simply cannot imagine it otherwise. When linguistic creations remain convincing with continued repetition, then they are spoken from true language; and the word that speaks for itself "even gains in strength of conviction by being passed from mouth to mouth, from generation to generation. A person always repeats with his own voice what the language has pronounced to him with its voice."[71]

3. We have examined changes in the linguistic thinking of our time from the most diverse points of view and have determined the following: As opposed to a clear disposition toward objectivity and information that has been especially prevalent in the modern period, one sees more strongly today the circular structure of language, which connects object and subject in an ever-new event and frees itself from the ideal of exactitude of earlier times. If one thought for a long time that language only portrayed what existed in nonlinguistic realms, then it has become clear today that language structures reality and, indeed, that only through language is a person in touch with reality. If language was seen earlier as essentially expression of the human inner life, then the consensus today is more and more that in regard to language, the human being is a recipient. If one believed earlier that the understandability of language could be clarified by means of the ever-constant and common nature of humanity, then we know today how much understanding is a function of relationship and community and thus of society. If one could earlier count on the certainty that linguistic development represented a constant onward and upward progression, then today attention has turned to exactly those areas that,

measured by the earlier idea of development, must have actually passed away and been overcome.

HEALING AS A LINGUISTIC EVENT

In the realm of pastoral care understood as proclamation there persists a downright baffling unanimity that a person must be understood in that view in a way basically different "from what is possible within the framework of spiritual questioning."[72] Even today, therefore, many theologians still deny that modern, anthropologically oriented medicine, with its "objectifying" methods, can grasp at all the totality and reality of the human being. And when the extension of secular anthropology into the inner disciplines is considered, this new consciousness is rejected as "overstepping the boundaries," in order to restrict the interpretation of the "true" human being to theology alone—consciously using a principle of exclusivity—and, in contrast to all of the provisional and peripheral efforts of psychotherapy, to bring into play the "last" and "genuine" healing power of pastoral care.[73] Dietrich Rössler holds this fateful attitude responsible for the often-lamented loss of touch with reality in today's pastoral care.[74]

Now, we must be prepared for a similar objection today when someone designates the word as the point of convergence of theology and psychology, as did Thomas Bonhoeffer, for example, in his inaugural lecture in Zurich.[75] Is not the word—it will be asked—of which theology speaks always qualified as the Word of God, which, as an objective quantity, strikes a person from the outside as the wholly other, while the word in psychotherapy remains the mutual speaking and responding of people entirely in the sphere of subjectivity? In what follows we will attempt to invalidate this objection with the help of an example that focuses attention on the central significance that should be accorded the linguistic event in the thinking of both theology and depth psychology and on the surprising parallels that result therefrom.

It is a wonder that the connection between healing and language has received so little attention in the past, since the whole of biblical linguistic usage assigns to the word a simply decisive healing function. When Ps. 107:20 says, "He sent forth his word, and healed them, and delivered them from destruction," and Wisd. of Sol. 16:12 reads, "For neither herb nor plaster heals, but your word, Lord, which heals all," they reflect the conceptual world of the Johannine proclamation, which, in the linking of word and life, places central importance on the healing significance of God's word (John 1:4; 5:26; 1 John 1:1ff.).[76] Also the healing reports in the Synoptic Gospels—in distinction to heathen magic and the vivid descriptions of possible individual methods that we find, say, in Plato—give prominence to Jesus' style of healing, which is accomplished essentially in the word (Mark 1:25–27, 40–41; 2:10–11; 5:41; 7:34; Matt. 8:8–13).[77]

The meaningful connection between word and healing, however, must have been lost very early, so that over the centuries and into our own day the biblical reports of healing have become a constantly new source of embarrassment for exegetes, although there has been no lack of ever-new attempts to reestablish that connection. Therefore, we shall look at one of these attempts, which was the work of a nineteenth-century figure from whom we are not separated by a long historical road: he is the Swabian pastor Johann Christoph Blumhardt.

Fifty years before Freud began to write case histories that, to his own amazement, read like novellas, Blumhardt had recorded the case history of Gottliebin Dittus, which immediately became a sensational best seller. Originally written as a confidential report to church authorities, it reached the public through an indiscretion and in a very short time was spread about in hundreds of copies that, in part, were substantially altered. Thus Blumhardt felt compelled to duplicate a limited number of copies of his authentic report. To this day, however, the original text has not succeeded in fully suppressing the wealth of circulating, sensationally dressed-up versions.[78]

At the beginning of her care from Blumhardt, Gottliebin Dittus was a twenty-eight-year-old woman, whose mother was apparently very talented; the parents died early and left five children in miserable financial circumstances. Since her childhood,

Gottliebin had known how, in one way or another, to make herself the central figure in the practice of magic, which was flourishing among the people.[79] She suffered from numerous illnesses, which had especially to do with the abdomen, and was therefore under constant medical treatment. She had been the declared favorite of Blumhardt's predecessor in Möttlingen, Dr. Barth, and the undisputed center of the soirees he arranged for young people. With the change in office, she lost this position, for Blumhardt found her distinctly unappealing. For Gottliebin the feeling was mutual: at Blumhardt's first sermon she had a strong desire to scratch out his eyes.[80] It is true that she went to the parsonage with the thoroughly unusual wish to confess, of her own free will, something of her past; but the relationship remained cool.[81] On Gottliebin's side there was an outspoken ambivalence. On the one hand, she was always there whenever Blumhardt spoke, even in the neighboring village at his other church; on the other hand, she manifested a depressed shyness and defensive reserve behind which Blumhardt suspected an exaggerated self-consciousness.

Nevertheless, Blumhardt was forced to have more dealings with Gottliebin when the house in which she lived became haunted. The main problem was repeated poltergeist noises, which Blumhardt, after an investigation with the village mayor, sought to bring to an end by abruptly evacuating the family. But then Gottliebin became sick with convulsions, which gave every sign of being what was customarily designated a little later as "grand hysteria" but which at the time left the attending physician totally perplexed. It was he who moved Blumhardt to make an even stronger effort in behalf of the sick woman when he said, "One would think there were no pastor around at all when the sick are left lying like that; this is not anything natural."[82] Now Blumhardt visited the sick woman frequently and became a witness to her spasms and convulsions. On a sudden impulse during one of these visits, he sprang onto the bed, seized Gottliebin's rigidly cramped hands, called her name, and said, "Hold your hands together and pray, 'Lord Jesus, help me.' We have seen what the devil does long enough; now we want to see also what the Lord Jesus can do."[83] With that, however, the real struggle began.

What had Blumhardt done with these words? He had given the pathological phenomena a particular interpretation that at first relieved the sick woman herself of any responsibility. It was, of course, the devil and the demons that were at work inside her, and thus she could give these powers the opportunity to articulate themselves, to be transposed into language.

For Blumhardt the decision to be made in those days was whether he should perhaps engage in some tricks of sympathy or exorcism, or whether he should remain with the word alone. He decided on the latter course and in that way endured the whole two-year struggle. In this connection it is characteristic that Blumhardt was raised in a theological tradition in which pastoral care could not consist in anything other than instruction and comforting. Language was employed in this authoritarian stance exclusively as information about the truths of faith. And this is exactly the way Blumhardt proceeded at first. He attempted a frontal assault on the illness by laying his hand on Gottliebin and repeating twelve times, one right after the other, "The Lord Jesus help you; the Lord Jesus preserve your body and your soul."[84] Or he repeated similar but no doubt suggestively effective formulas. The decisive turning point, which caused Blumhardt to give up this instrumental use of language and the word, came when Gottliebin so identified with the demons who seemed to possess her that they spoke out of her. At this point Blumhardt decided, after careful consideration, to take what was, for the practice of pastoral care at that time, the unusual step of entering "into a discreetly held dialogue."[85] With that the situation changed decisively, because everything that tormented and preyed upon Gottliebin could find linguistic expression and was interpretively received by Blumhardt.

Thus, fifty years before Freud developed his techniques, we see here already the archetype of psychotherapeutic dialogue suggestively realized. It is also, therefore, not at all astonishing that the main themes that were now articulated in the form of language are the same themes that are well known to every psychotherapist. Foremost was the sexual theme: Gottliebin could now admit that every Wednesday and Friday she was "raped" by evil spirits to the point of heavy genital bleeding.[86] There was enslavement by feelings of guilt for evil deeds of the past. There was the theme of sadomasochism: the "demons" repeatedly threatened to become aggressive against Blumhardt and others, they gleefully reported on earthquakes and great conflagrations like that in Hamburg where they were present as eye witnesses, and finally everything was directed toward tormenting Gottliebin herself to the point of extremely demonstrative suicide attempts. Especially noteworthy is the restless search of the "demons" who kept Gottliebin possessed for an object they could safely relate to, for they repeatedly asked Blumhardt whether she might not find a place of rest in his house.[87] Thus it was certainly not by accident that Gottliebin's final healing was sealed by her being accepted as a child into Blumhardt's family, where she developed into an indispensable right hand in Blumhardt's further work—which led the psychiatrist Viktor von Weizsäcker to remark that the real winner of Blumhardt's struggle was Gottliebin. The formula that, for Blumhardt, could banish with one stroke all of the ghosts and demons and, psychologically speaking, mobilize the forces of ego integration was the cry "Jesus is victor." Perhaps one could also draw on this fact as an exposition in actual experience of Jung's formulation, for which he was criticized again and again, that Christ can be understood as a symbol of the self.

Blumhardt himself never even dreamed of attempting a psychological interpretation of his experiences. His language was the thoroughly mythological language of the Bible, to which he naively saw himself contemporaneous. What he did on the basis of this spirituality can, nevertheless, be incorporated without difficulty into a context of meaning understandable today as soon as one has found a suitable conceptual framework. As is well known, Rudolf Bultmann held the conceptual system of Heidegger's existential philosophy to be especially suitable for his program of demythologization. It is extremely characteristic, however, that this conceptual system had to fail in Blumhardt's case. Bultmann could only hold the Blumhardt stories up to the suspicion of absurdity or push them aside with angry emotion. He repeatedly emphasized that for him they were an abomination.

Only depth psychology makes available a conceptual framework that enables us to understand the Blumhardt phenomenon. This understanding can be summarized as follows:

1. Blumhardt apparently discovered a form of linguistic intercourse with the ill that expands the instrumental character of language as pure suggestion, instruction, or comforting into the dialogical structure of genuine discussion.

2. This makes it possible to give a name to alien, sinister powers felt within oneself and to help them articulate themselves.

3. The illness moves thereby out of the realm of pure fate and into the realm of human responsibility as soon as the demons are deposed and, through the power of Jesus' name, subjected to the rule of the ego. Blumhardt resolutely extended this experience with spiritual illness also to all bodily ills and could make the statement that a drop of determined resistance against illness was worth more to him than a whole sea of surrender. Thus he can rightly be addressed as one of the progenitors of the psychosomatic point of view.

4. For Blumhardt the possibilities of communication through language allowed liberation from the past to be realized and freedom for the future to shine forth in a meaningful and life-promoting community of love.

Exactly parallel to this is the reshaping of the relationship between doctor and patient undertaken by Freud. It is shown best by the fact that the first tentative efforts to incorporate linguistic communication into medical science actually took place in a completely nonlinguistic fashion. Bypassing the circular structure that is characteristic of language and dialogue, hypnosis was used as a means of switching off the patient's conscious mind and achieving the immediacy of instruction and command suggestively and directly in the unconscious. Freud had learned this method in Paris from Jean-Martin Charcot and discovered very early its inadequacy. That is, it by no means brought freedom to the patient but replaced servitude under the power of the illness with servitude under the power of the doctor. The curing of the symptoms lasted only as long as the doctor was incorporated into the life of the patient as a continuing institution, whether he became part of the fabric of instinctual wishes or whether he assumed the position of the superego authority. Because of these distressing results of experiments with the so-called cathartic method, Freud's colleague Josef Breuer withdrew completely from this research. Yet Freud did not give up at this point. His aim was to place at his patients' disposal the greatest possible amount of room for freedom and thereby return to them their capacity for work and enjoyment. He was probably the first to recognize that a person must accomplish the freedom that had become his lot in the modern period, not only outwardly in nature and in the social structure; he himself must also stubbornly force this freedom out of himself by driving his consciousness as far as possible into the realm of his own unconscious. Freud reduced this effort to a short, precise formula: What was id, shall become ego. In his spirit we can add, What was superego, shall also become ego.

With great astonishment Freud discovered it did not appear as self-evident to people as one might assume that this freedom was a good thing worth striving for. His psychoanalytical treatment proceeded as a sheer battle between analyst and patient within which the patient wanted to act out his problems, that is, wanted to assign the analyst the role of a commanding, directive-giving, authoritative personage, while the analyst wanted to submit the problems to thoughtful consideration. Freud immediately saw that it was a great temptation to the analyst to step into this authority role, to influence the patient by suggestion, and to shape and "ennoble" him after the analyst's own image.[88] All of these wishes and longings had to be denied the patient in psychoanalytical treatment. There was only one possibility: to understand them and through interpretation to let the patient share in this understanding.

The authority of the analyst did not relieve the patient of the ethical decision that he had to make; rather, the interpretation presented to him a kind of preliminary understanding, which the analyst had found by means of his theory and with which he could give the patient names for as yet unconscious relationships, which were thereby given back to the patient for responsible decision. The directions in which the understanding had to press forward were twofold. On the one hand, the patient's individual life history had to be discussed. The patient had to learn to admit to himself what he had done and to acknowledge to himself how he really was. He could not begin with an ideal image of what a person ought to be; he had to start with the reality of how he was. On the other hand, however, the understanding had to be broadened in the direction of tradition. The later Freud had to admit that a human being, in his unconscious, participates somehow in the ancient heritage of humanity. He is not freed from that tradition simply because it is no longer taught to him; he is still bound to it through his unconscious.[89] The symbols appearing in dreams and other productions of the unconscious are therefore to be tested to see what binding power they still hold for the present moment. Freud achieved this with his method of dream interpretation, which in no way consisted in interpreting symbolically encoded messages with a dictionary, as it were, but consisted in first assigning to them an initial, preliminary understanding that originated from the ideas associated with the dream by the patient and from the sphere of everyday life. The preliminary understanding of the free associations smoothed the way to a final interpretation, so that in the end decisions could grow out of that dialectical movement between tradition and personal individuality. The hierarchical structure of directive and obedience is thereby replaced by the dialogical, circular structure of understanding.

What are the results of our considerations for the practice of counseling?

1. In a dialogue neither of the two partners has the lead. Speaking and responding cause the dialogue to move forward without carrying out a previously determined agenda. This process expresses the partnership and mutuality of the dialogue.

2. Nonetheless, in the model psychotherapeutic dialogue a

certain asymmetry obtains because of the interpretation that the therapist tries to give his partner. On the one hand, these interpretations give names and objectify, but on the other hand, they do not objectify, in that they are given back to the patient for verification or falsification with an intentional and fundamental readiness for modification.

3. In a dialogue thus understood, the achievement of a little bit of freedom has to be accomplished not only vis-à-vis nature and authority but also in regard to oneself.

4. Through dialogue decisive aid is given toward exercising this freedom. For when one succeeds through dialogue in changing feelings and sentiments into words, this means an undoubted increase in freedom from bondage to instincts. If dialogue reigns in the sexual relationship between a man and a woman, the relationship is not in danger of slipping down into areas where neither partner can any longer be responsible. Above all, responsible relations between the sexes consist in the practice of dialogue. Likewise, it can be noted that through dialogue the tendencies of aggressive drives can be restrained and changed into reasonable formulations and concrete actions. This has been observed especially in cases of student unrest where opposing sides, through persistent discussion, have finally found reasonable and practical courses of action that were impossible to determine or derive on the basis of unbridled aggressiveness.

5. Dialogue can thus be designated as the wellspring of ethical decision. In it possibilities are revealed that had occurred to neither of the two partners previously, yet this is something that can happen in every counseling session. Whether dialogue can become a structural element within the church might be a crucial question for the manifestation of life in this institution. Our recommendation is to see at precisely this point the pastoral element in ecclesiastical activity.

2. Basic Forms of Dialogue

THESIS: Dialogue presupposes full equality between the two partners but allows a certain specification of roles and concentration of effort. A complete symmetry of roles exists only in the *open dialogue.* A shifting of roles in one direction or another occurs in the *teaching dialogue,* the limits of which come into view when it tries to work suggestively, or in the *exploratory dialogue,* which is only a dialogue as long as its results are not objectified into a diagnosis. A combination of these two possibilities is attempted in the *helping relationship* as it is practiced in modern social work. The *pastoral dialogue* does not represent a special form of dialogue alongside the others but, rather, makes use of all four of the forms named, although it is oriented especially toward the helping relationship, which it tries to interpret on the level of understanding of that which is of ultimate concern to the individual.

We have tried to clarify the basic elements of dialogue by examining the execution of language itself. As criteria for what can be understood as dialogue we presented the equality of the two partners that can lead to nonauthoritarian interchange, the enabling and exercising of freedom, and the circular structure of the reciprocation of language between two or more participants. We must now ask what shifts of emphasis can occur within the framework thus delineated and where the boundaries of what we can still designate as dialogue are. Therefore, as the ideal type of dialogue, we will first look at what can be called the open dialogue. It is conceived as an absolute partnership and is absolutely symmetrical in its structure. It is completely removed from manipulation, and characteristic of it is something like a happening. Nonetheless, the open dialogue always has a result. It is that hard-to-describe feeling of satisfaction that befalls one when regarding a work of art if one has the impression that this piece of art "works." Thus the boundary of the open dialogue might lie at the point where such a feeling of satisfaction does not result but, rather, the dialogue becomes an absolute end in itself, is completely without result, and is thus senseless.

Now, it seems thoroughly compatible with the reciprocal equality that we saw as fundamental in every dialogue to say, however, that the concentration of effort can shift between the two partners in the dialogue. This is doubtless the case in the teaching dialogue, which is, therefore, no longer recognized by many as a dialogue at all in the true sense of the word.[1] Thus, Otto Friedrich Bollnow questions whether, besides the pastoral and the therapeutic dialogue, the teaching dialogue also has the character of a dialogue in the strict sense. He claims that the intent to educate necessarily sets equality aside and that for this intent it is the very superiority of the one, the teaching partner, that is important.[2] In the following we will attempt to show how a dialogue more strongly oriented toward teaching can, nevertheless, take place as an equality-preserving partnership. According to our established criteria, the boundary could be drawn, perhaps, at the point where the teaching dialogue no longer respects the partner's freedom and tries consciously or unconsciously to work suggestively. We saw earlier that giving up a psychotherapy that works by suggestion is precisely what creates the possibility of dialogue in the true sense of the word.

The symmetry of the dialogue can also become skewed in the opposite direction. Then the personality of the dialogue partner receives a certain emphasis, whether he comes with a special concern or a problem, or whether it is a question of providing him with an understanding of his own situation. Such a dialogue would then more definitely have the character of making clear to both partners particular information that contains the key to understanding the other person and his special situation.

It would have the character of an exploratory dialogue. Of course, when such an undertaking is carried out with the decided intention of later forming an objective diagnosis—whether in regard to fundamental characteristics of the dialogue partner or his suitability for certain tasks or even in the psychopathological sense—then, it seems to us, one has left the realm of what we are willing to designate as dialogue.

Only with hesitation has acceptance in our land been gained by the principles of what the English-speaking world calls social casework. Here, however, it is the very relationship between the two partners in the dialogue that can exercise a helping function. As far as I can see, there is still, in the German-language literature, a total failure to take note of the immediate proximity of this helping relationship to what pastoral care could be, although in the United States, for example, this has been entirely a matter of course for decades. Perhaps also playing a more or less conscious role here is that curious hierarchical structure of thinking within our academic establishment which only with difficulty can bring itself to allow a function generally practiced by nonacademics to become a model for an academic profession like that of the pastor. Yet one should finally take cognizance of the fact that an extraordinarily diligent and discriminating analysis of dialogical processes has been made available here, and compared with it, the authoritarian and methodical techniques that are offered for pastoral dialogue can only be termed clumsy and coarse. Therefore, it seems to me extraordinarily fruitful to examine the methods of the helping relationship in regard to its underlying basic principles and to investigate whether hidden therein might lie possibilities for helping to bring pastoral care into closer accord with reality, of which it apparently is in great need if it is ever to have a chance worth mentioning for the future. At this point we must ask what alternatives are available if we can no longer understand pastoral dialogue in the sense of proclamation.

THE OPEN DIALOGUE

The unanimous experience of all who are involved in any kind of social interchange seems to be that what we would like to call the open dialogue does not let itself be planned, compelled, or manipulated. It happens without our readily perceiving the conditions under which it is possible. Because of this "happening" character of the dialogue, a person in our day also perceives himself primarily as a recipient. It is an experience similar to the everyday experiences of falling asleep—which also cannot be compelled by the will—of dreaming, and having creative ideas. Now, in present-day theological discussion there seems to have been a reestablishment of the custom of bringing up the word "mystery" and seeing here a sign of God's work. I cite Gerhard Ebeling: "Whenever it concerns a person at the point of being a recipient, of living life as a gift, as grace, of being surrounded by mystery, then this is a pointer toward understanding, a hint of what it means to be the concern of God."[3] In my opinion, such a theological interpretation of a basic everyday experience of human existence seems to be legitimate only if the term "mystery" does not seduce one into a suspension of critical thinking, which, with a mild theological shudder, retreats before the possibility that one can still discover certain psychologically comprehensible regularities even behind this boundary line marked by human openness. We will most certainly have to hold on to the insight that the open dialogue, just like sleep, dreams, and creative ideas, cannot be compelled by the will. But this does not mean that we cannot gain some insight into what factors play a role in determining whether such an open dialogue succeeds or fails. Since depth psychology has crossed over the boundary of psychological research that seemed to have been set by consciousness, we know something of the psychic effects coming from a realm that is not subject to the conscious control of the will. Thus the unconscious operation of the psyche can be made responsible for a dialogue's occurring between two or more participants, as well as for the barriers that can stand in its way. Simplifying, we can perhaps say that the stronger the unconscious communication between the participants is, the stronger will be the possibility of what we call the open dialogue. On the other hand, the more that one or more participants are cut off from their own unconscious, the less likely it will be that a dialogue can take place. Through what observation can this somewhat apodictically operating thesis be supported?

No one will question the fact that for the coming-about of a dialogue, mutual understanding is of decisive importance. The progress of understanding, nonetheless, can be quite severely hindered by a process that psychoanalysis has uncovered and circumscribed with the label "repression." To the extent that someone finds it necessary to alienate himself from certain areas of his own unconscious—that is, to keep them from becoming conscious—he will not be in a position to understand those areas with another person and to accept them. On the contrary, he will continually project what he cannot acknowledge about himself onto the other person and attack it there. This can be easily demonstrated with literary examples.[4] Repression is therefore one of the great foes of the open dialogue, and one can flatly state that cultural epochs or social structures within which a great deal must be repressed must also be regarded as distinctly hostile to dialogue. Within a system that can extol obedience as the only cardinal virtue, no dialogue can develop; over the centuries the Prussian tradition with its rule of "Shut your mouth and obey!" knew precisely where to place this accent so hostile to dialogue. Perhaps it is not entirely unimportant to make clear that the force in our time that is repressive and thus hostile to dialogue emanates not only from those circles that seek to erect a "dictatorship of decency." There are also those who under the cloak of a certain mock liberality and using clichéd concepts and models work against the articulation of the individual unconscious by seeking to describe very exactly how feelings are to occur and to be articulated in today's world.

When one must repress, one also gives up the possibility of sharing in the unconscious side of a particular situation in time. One's means of expression will then be peculiarly lacking in general understandability. At this point the language of many theologians could provide impressive illustration. Finally, we must also consider that through repression a person alienates himself from what Freud called the archaic heritage of humanity, which, with Jung, we could call the collective unconscious and which, as long as human history lasts, continually gives off its energies and sets us free. Every poetic creation draws from that unconscious portion of the soul.

Are we thus trying to say that total consciousness seems to offer the ideal precondition for dialogue? This is indeed the opinion that is supposed to be represented here. Of course, we must also consider the fact that such is not a possibility in the historical existence of humanity. One could, indeed, also regard the dynamic of the historical process as the incessant giving-off of energies from the realm of the unconscious. When the unconscious has completely released its energies, the end of history will be here, the human person will be fully identical with himself, he will see "face to face," and the eschaton will have arrived. It seems to me that the enthusiast movements of all epochs have taken this basic fact of human existence too little into account. Those who intend to reach total consciousness through enlightenment will regularly be in danger of catching themselves again in the snare of the still-present unconscious and seeing revolutionary efforts toward becoming conscious sink into unconscious and irrational emotions. Thus, in what we are striving to do here, it cannot be a question of an enthusiast anticipation of the eschatological vastness of a total consciousness but is rather the question whether we can reach and fulfill the level of consciousness appropriate to our historical situation. This means above all, however, reversing and making understandable the mechanism of repression that has such an unhealthy effect on the development of dialogue.

Hence, we can make understandable in outline form those factors that stand in the way of the development of open dialogue. They are certainly not to be sought on the level of intelligence and vocabulary. There are also open dialogues between people who have at their disposal neither a high intelligence quotient nor a richly differentiated vocabulary. Poor conditions for the development of dialogue are no doubt created, however, whenever a person, through drill and training, is raised to passivity, when his critical faculty is placed into a state of permanent inattention by the mild narcotic of certain styles of writing, speaking, and even preaching. One is rendered incapable of dialogue by one's own blind spots that come into being during the process of repression. When repression reaches the point where we must speak of the condition of neurosis, the communication begins to take place on two levels: we receive from the other person linguistic signals that, in addition to their generally accessible meaning, also have another secret code meaning. Thus, for example, someone might open up a pastoral counseling session, which he has sought with great persistence, by saying, "I'm sure you have a lot more important things to do than to talk to me." And the secret meaning of this opening statement is an earnest plea for a certain amount of attention and concern. In cases where it finally comes to a complete overflowing of the unconscious—as it might, say, in psychosis—an unrestrained stream of language is indeed often released, but we stand by helpless because we can no longer decipher the meaning of these words.

The circular nature of our situation is demonstrated by the fact that there is apparently no other effective means of clearing away these hindrances than through dialogue itself. As Bollnow has so rightly noted, it is a question not only of helping a person through dialogue but, together with that, of making him able and ready for dialogue in the first place.[5]

Which factors, then, are the ones that can arouse the feeling of satisfaction after an open dialogue which we described earlier? For one thing, there is another person's understanding acceptance of what is said.[6] Second is the fact that formulation into language "contributes substantially to the clarification of what is oppressing the person concerned in a way that is confusing and in this confusion threatening."[7] Through the mutuality of the reflection a greater degree of consciousness is reached. There comes a liberation from objective bias, a dissolving of one's own prejudice and errors, in short, what Bollnow calls a critical cleansing.[8]

As one of the most decisive arguments against the development of dialogue someone is always trotting out the fact that the people of our hectic age have no more time for dialogue.

Nonetheless, it can be easily demonstrated that behind the question of dealing with time lies the question of people dealing with themselves and also particularly with their unconscious regions; and thus one can venture the thesis that the person who is not in tune with himself also has no time at his disposal. The problem of time is thereby also revealed as a phenomenon of repression.

THE TEACHING DIALOGUE

We have proposed to show that the possibility of an instructional communication of knowledge also lies within the mutual equality of the dialogue. For this to be realized, it seems that there are two historical prerequisites. On the one hand is the critical thrust against the unbroken passing down of traditions through the elders. This thrust can burst forth at certain times and express itself, for example, in the following sentence: "The times are over in which the elders directed everything and served as guardians: we young people must ourselves take our affairs in hand, for we, indeed, bear all the consequences." The quotation comes from the sophist Trasymachos in the fourth century B.C.[9]

The other historical presupposition is the conviction that what is happening in the instruction is not the passing-on of completely new information but rather the latent self-recollection of personal experiences. As Werner Jäger has impressively demonstrated, this conviction, which led to the development of the Socratic method, is to be found expressed for the first time in the Hippocratic literature of ancient medicine.[10] Here the criterion for the truth of a doctor's opinion is whether it can be brought into agreement with the anamnesis of the patient.[11] The mark of the Socratic teaching dialogue is, therefore, not the overpowering of alien views "but the awakening of unborn knowledge still sleeping within the self. The birth of this sleeping knowledge comes in a roundabout way through the insight of the instructed one into his own ignorance."[12]

Erwin Metzke offers a description of the Socratic teaching dialogue:

> Socrates knew that he did not know. Precisely this he saw as the essence of his wisdom, which turned him into a questioner. This ignorance is the basic element of his dialogical method. . . . His dialogue always begins with his analyzing supposed claims to knowledge—supposed knowledge—and melting them down in the fire of his critical questions. . . . Whoever believes that he knows already has from the outset closed the gate through which knowledge can enter. . . . The first step in Socrates' guidance of dialogue is, therefore, marked by "irony": the ironic exposing of supposed knowledge as ignorance. The second step, however, is not at all the formulation of an answer; Socrates seeks, rather, to guide a person to the insight that he truly must always gain knowledge himself, that it can never be conveyed from the outside as pure knowledge.[13]

Thus one can say that Socrates wanted not to influence but to allow a person to gain insights himself; therefore, he did not want to work suggestively. He wanted to release the free, living, independent response of the other person. He wanted to let the other person find the answer himself.[14] As Jäger shows, knowledge is thus rooted "in a deep layer of the soul in which the pervasion of knowledge and the possession of the known are no longer to be separated but are essentially one."[15] Thus, here the unconscious realm is completely drawn in as the actually creative part of a person and not shielded by repression. Hence, a teaching dialogue thus understood has the function of opening up for a person the possibility of creative inspiration.

In this way, however, there comes a widening of the area of consciousness. "Education in the Socratic sense becomes the striving toward philosophically conscious life formation that is aimed at the goal of fulfilling the spiritual and moral destiny of a person."[16] A teaching dialogue thus understood is, therefore, not at all in conflict with human freedom; on the contrary, it seeks to accomplish this freedom: "What concerned Socrates was apparently not pure independence from whatever norms exist outside the individual but the effectiveness of the control that the person himself exercises over his own being. Thereby a new concept of inner freedom developed."[17] With this formulation a concern was touched that fulfilled itself centuries later in psychoanalysis.

It is important to keep in mind that this type of teaching dialogue may have been maintained only with Socrates and that with Plato it already experienced an important revision. For, as both Metzke and Jäger are able to show, the dialogues of Plato to an increasing extent presuppose a "knowing one who leads the learning one to the truth."[18] Plato already speaks as a teacher who in the end is himself no longer called into question. Therefore, the figure of Socrates in the dialogues withdraws more and more, and into his place steps Parmenides, the teacher and proclaimer of being. In this way the Platonic teaching dialogue breaks away from mutual reciprocity. The level of equality is abandoned. The dialogue is ruled by a suggestive power which, to be sure, stimulates active common reflection, but which, on the other hand, is marked by the methodological certainty with which the dialogue is led.[19] Apparently—but only apparently—these dialogues do not go beyond the Socratic ignorance. In them an advance toward an objective becomes clear, a "guiding strategic spirit that directs the whole power of its attack on the one question: What is the nature of this knowledge?"[20]

It was important to me to clarify with typical examples the radical change that occurred within what can be understood as a teaching dialogue. It would be fascinating to follow this development through Western history. I would like to try to pinpoint only the final stage of this development, and I would like to do that with a classical formulation that was coined a hundred years ago and that seems not to have lost any of its relevance today:

> A talking mouth and very many ears with half as many writing hands—that is the external academic apparatus; that is the educational machine of the university set into motion. Moreover, the proprietor of this mouth is separated from and not dependent on the owners of the many ears; and this double independence is praised with exultation as "academic freedom." Incidentally—to lift up this freedom again—the one can say more or less what he will; the other hear more or less what he will: only that behind both groups, at a modest distance, stands the state with a certain anxious supervisory countenance in order to remind from time to time

that it (the state) is the purpose and goal and essence of the curious speaking and hearing procedure.[21]

THE EXPLORATORY DIALOGUE

If the symmetry of the dialogue shifts in the other direction, the dialogue takes on more decidedly the character of an exploration. According to Ludwig Pongratz, the dialogue encounter enables us to see the shape of the personality and, in particular, its movement in the context of an encounter with a fellow human being, in its living, active manifestation to a personal thou. Accordingly, one could call the exploration an active inquiry.[22] In the process, it is important that such a dialogue have the task of judging not the dialogue partner—this would be an objectifying manner—but, rather, the overall course of a social partnership, to the formation of which both partners contribute substantially.[23] With the setting of the task of observing these proceedings, of course, an "asymmetrical social situation" is created,[24] but the difference in roles does not prevent the encounter and allows very well for reciprocal equality.[25] The asymmetry of such a dialogue expresses itself in the fact that the explorer seeks to devote himself to a completely passive role, while he strives to leave the active role to the one being explored. It is the unanimous experience of those who have attempted such dialogues that in the course of such a discussion the one being explored slowly seeks to reverse this asymmetry, tries to gain power over the interviewer, and strives to shift to him the active role. The dynamics of this process must always be kept in mind.[26] The reciprocal equality consists in the fact that during such a dialogue the personality of the leader, in its peculiarity and essential structure, is an operating factor in the dialogue and one that cannot be eliminated. Therefore, the dialogue presupposes a certain critical self-evaluation. If it is neglected, then it will sneak in again and again as the one great source of errors.[27] Thus, in such a dialogue, one must absolutely hold to the basic realization that what is being analyzed is not a personality but a dialogue. It is a question of a psychic field of action that is determined by three factors:

(*a*) the goal set for the dialogue
(*b*) the one being questioned
(*c*) the one who is leading the dialogue[28]

So that this basic given will not be lost from sight, Ulrich Moser recommends that the counselor ask himself several questions at the beginning of the dialogue:

1. Why is the counselee coming? (On his own initiative? Because of a third party? Under some kind of pretext?)
2. Why is he coming to me, and how did he get my name?
3. What significance does he have for me, and what role will he perhaps play in my unconscious fantasies?
4. In what spiritual situation must I carry out the dialogue?
5. What impression does the counselee want to make?
6. What expectations will he have in regard to my thoughts and feelings?[29]

Not until the social situation to be observed is clarified in this way can one turn to the question of which areas of possible importance for the foundation of a pastoral dialogue can be investigated in such an exploratory dialogue. I would like to order them into four groups:

(*a*) social behavior
(*b*) biographical data
(*c*) the question of mental illness
(*d*) behavior of the partner in the dialogue

Yet we must in any case avoid the misunderstanding that the items just listed can be organized into a kind of questionnaire that can be systematically completed during an exploratory dialogue. The captions can have at most the status of a critical self-examination after such an exploratory dialogue and serve rather as a mnemonic aid for what I perhaps might have to experience in later sessions.

Social behavior. In order to understand the situation of a person who comes with a special concern or a conflict, I will have to learn something about the people to whom he relates. At this point, to be sure, one must be especially discreet with questions, for it is often very characteristic which family members are mentioned scarcely or not at all. For social behavior it is also characteristic which stereotypical judgments the counselee may express even in the first session and perhaps repeat later on. Above all, I will have to pay attention to whether there are, within the social contacts of the counselee, typical patterns, that is, whether he appears to experience the same thing again and again.

Biographical data. We need not give special emphasis to the fact that the mother-child relationship can possibly be a characteristic weak point for the whole of later life. Also important for a person's response to events is very often the birth order as well as especially aggravating childhood diseases and childhood anxieties. The phase of early childhood sexuality can never be interrogated in the first session but deserves special attention if it is mentioned. With the beginning of school the problem of achievement enters the field of interest, and there are often extraordinarily characteristic patterns of achievement. How puberty was experienced and felt as well as the choices of occupation and mate provide further important indications. Here too it will again be very important to ascertain—and not hinder the exploration through questions—whether the counselee skips over certain stages in his life and especially emphasizes particular themes such as vocation, illnesses, money, or sexuality. One must always keep in mind that in such an exploratory dialogue what matters is not at all an exact, precise, detailed knowledge of the person's life history but rather—in Pongratz's felicitous expression—the history of experience: "The how of a life event is more important than the what. For it is not the what that is individual, but the how."[30]

Mental illness. For the initiation of a pastoral counseling relationship it appears to be extremely important that, through a dialogue oriented toward exploration, one achieve clarity from the very beginning on the point of whether the counselee's problem concerns a mental illness or whether his mental health is basically stable. Any unqualified intrusion into a psychically pathological process can, naturally, have extremely harmful consequences for the counselee. For our purposes it will suffice to distinguish two categories of mental illnesses: on the one hand, the psychosis, and on the other, the neurosis. With a psychosis it is a question of a mental sickness that generally goes back to a constitutionally given factor (heredity) and an as yet not completely researched physical event. The most striking symptoms are that the person hears voices, that he has feelings of alienation vis-à-vis other people and experiences strange bodily sensations and even systematic delusions that in the initial stages are frequently not very easy to recognize. It appears hopeless to enter into a discussion with a deluded person about his delusions. Nor may one reinforce him in his delusions. Every psychotic illness belongs in the hands of a psychiatrist. If one wants to be involved as a pastor in further care of the person, then this absolutely must take place in consultation with a psychiatrist.

To be distinguished from psychoses are neuroses, which basically consist in an intrapsychical conflict event stemming from early childhood. They are manifested in bodily ailments without organic foundation, in certain compulsions, or in anxieties related to objects that otherwise do not instill fear. As a rule the decisive role in the formation of a neurosis is played by sexual repression. Therefore, with a normal sexual development, there is rarely a neurosis. Neurotic illnesses belong in the hands of a trained psychotherapist. For a referral to such an expert, three criteria are indispensable:

1. Does the person have an understanding of his illness?
2. Is he under a burden of suffering?
3. Is the will to recover present?

Only when these three criteria are met will referrals to a psychotherapist be promising. Any surreptitious or deviously arranged contact with a therapist must be regarded as ineffectual from the beginning.

Behavior in the dialogue. Finally, as the most important aspect of the exploratory dialogue, the behavior of the dialogue partner must be kept in mind. We must ask ourselves what role he is playing and what role he wants to give to the pastor. In asking these questions we must, above all else, consider the extent to which the behavior of the counselee and the role he has for the pastor are separated from reality. The more illusionary the expectations of the counselee are, the more infantile his own demeanor is, and the more overpowering the role is that he wants to give us, then the more disturbed will be his psychic situation.

In the realm of the pastoral dialogue we will see the significance of a more exploratorily defined dialogue in the clarification of the following questions:

1. In the case of this counselee, is it a question of mental illness?
2. Is it a question of a conflict? This conflict can take place on three levels:
   (*a*) within himself to the point of considerable immaturity
   (*b*) in relation to another person
   (*c*) with the social order in general

Above all, such an exploratory dialogue should attempt to clarify on which level the main problem lies; whether it deals mainly with a question of insight, so that here a teaching dialogue would be helpful; whether it is rather a question of understanding one's own situation or the situation of another, in which case the dialogue should offer help in understanding; or whether, finally, it is a question of personal maturity, for which the "helping relationship"—developed in social work and to be presented below—seems especially appropriate.

In a dialogue understood primarily as exploration, I will leave the sphere of what can still be understood as dialogue in that moment when I concern myself with objectifying the results into a diagnosis. At this point insurmountable difficulties will arise, to the extent that there persists an unusually strong skepticism—probably also justified from the psychological viewpoint—as to whether a dialogue can be employed at all as a useful means of reaching a diagnosis.[31]

THE HELPING RELATIONSHIP

The helping relationship represents in a certain sense a combination of two basic types of dialogue already described, the teaching dialogue and the exploratory dialogue. Reminiscent of the teaching dialogue as we presented it is the concerted effort of the helping relationship to make the client as independent as possible in regard to his total life style.[32] Its task can be paraphrased as follows: "Help toward self-help has the task of leading the client to a better self-understanding, a more mature consciousness of his internal and external life situation, so that in the future he can help himself."[33] What already came into view by way of suggestion in the discussion of the exploratory dialogue, namely, the importance of the interpersonal relationship, now moves completely to the fore. According to a classical definition by M. Bower, this "social casework" is defined as the "art through which the knowledge of science about human relationships and training in dealing with relationships is employed to mobilize abilities in the individual and, moreover, to open up community resources that are suited to bringing about a better adjustment of the client to the whole or to part of his environment."[34] The helping relationship can, therefore, be designated plainly as the observing of the dynamic interaction of attitudes and feelings between the social worker and the client.[35] In the dialogue situation the social worker has the following functions: (*a*) speaking, (*b*) listening, (*c*) pausing, (*d*) observing.[36]

The decisive point, however, is what this observing is directed toward. It is, namely, not at all directed primarily toward the client: the subtlest tool of the social worker includes a part of his own being, his feelings, his ideas. By trying to make himself conscious of this part of his own being, he can succeed in using these resources in a way that can lead to seeking and finding, together with the other person, an approach to solving the current difficulties.[37] Here we see translated into methodological practice the hermeneutical principle that there can be no objective or objectifying observation among human beings. Only the fact that the same drives and forces, the same ways of behaving are also present as possibilities within himself gives the social worker the empathy and imagination that lead him to learn understanding.[38] Self-observation, together with constant practice in unbiased thinking, and the perfection of an accepting inner attitude that does not depreciate and condemn people—these are regarded as the foundation of this modern branch of social work.[39] It should be clear that attention is directed to one's own person not for the purpose of placing special importance on one's own feelings but rather for the very purpose of being able to subtract them, as it were, from the helping relationship. It should be immediately apparent that this is a difficult requirement. Nonetheless, methods have been discovered that will offer help here too. One is a certain self-checking through subsequent evaluation of each session; another is supervision. We will deal with both of these possibilities later.[40]

For the client the helping relationship becomes a kind of model experience. Since the participation of another person in our life, his understanding, his affirmation and concern, his interest and his care all meet a primal need in every person, the methodology of the helping relationship relies on the inclination of people to satisfy this primal need. Thereby, however, the social worker is accorded a completely new kind of authority, in the exercise of which he injects himself, not in an improper fashion, into the life of a person; yet this authority creates the possibility that the client will have the new experience of a positive relationship. With that, there is the justifiable hope that what the client has "practiced" in this way with the social worker he will also succeed in doing later with another person.[41] A further important point in the basic principles of the helping relationship is that in all circumstances one avoids making demands at the beginning of a contact. The basic principle is, rather, that the experience of emotional satisfaction must in every case precede demands for achievement. The principle may be expressed thus: first, it is a question of promoting mental and physical capabilities; then, perhaps, achievement can also be demanded.[42]

Now, if we ask ourselves what the means are with which one works in this helping relationship, we can summarize with the following points: The help toward self-help is first of all moved by the conviction of the client's own powers of development. This conviction must be conveyed to him. Second, this method works with constructive questions. Third, it involves a rather sparing use of advice. Fourth, it concentrates on recognizing and exploiting every possibility of handing over independent decisions to the client. Fifth, one exercises the greatest restraint in expressing one's own opinions. And sixth, one tries to reach the right level of one's own activity.[43]

What, then, are the basic scientific and spiritual convictions that stand behind what we have come to know as the helping relationship? As scientific convictions, the following points can be mentioned:

(*a*) the topical viewpoint of the human psyche, that is, the conviction, developed in psychoanalysis, of the psychic structure of the ego, the id, and the superego, and also the method of operation of psychic defense mechanisms
(*b*) the significance of the emotional life for adjustment and the significance of interpersonal relationships for the success of the adjustment process
(*c*) the possibilities for behavioral changes and their causes
(*d*) the theories that have been developed and articulated around the concepts of status and role[44]

As essential ideas in social casework the following things are also mentioned in recent publications: love of neighbor, the concept of social justice, the idea of the solidarity and equality of all people before God, the concept of the uniqueness and worth of the individual person, the idea of human freedom and responsibility as well as the human potential for change.[45]

This very precisely and distinctly developed methodology of dealing with people is thus carried out with a definite human attitude that is marked by the aspects of acceptance, toleration, and encouragement. The goal to be strived for is the strengthening of the ego, that is, the conscious and free person of the partner.[46]

THE NATURE OF THE PASTORAL DIALOGUE

If we now raise the question of the character of the pastoral dialogue, it may be difficult in an additive process to bestow on it a special role and special status. In the open dialogue, the teaching dialogue, the exploratory dialogue, and above all the helping relationship, there are elements that correspond to the basic event of faith. If we want to speak of an analogy between the role of the pastor and that which he represents, then certainly we would use not the analogy of the dignity with which the greatness of the task is to be made clear (Asmussen) but rather, if anything, the analogy of the cross, through which the personality of the pastor, and therewith the relationship, is given so much attention that he can be subtracted from the situation. A person can become aware of what concerns him ultimately not because of the magnitude of the personal dignity of the pastor but perhaps because of the way the pastor attempts to make himself superfluous and to allow the other person his freedom. It seems to me, therefore, completely impossible, in considering the question of the pastoral dialogue, to think of two spheres separated from each other—as this has been attempted again and again in the present day—so that one believes that all of a person's problems of adjustment with his environment and even with himself can be turned over to secular institutions, and it is only a question of making a diagnosis to determine whether the person has a problem of adjustment vis-à-vis God, that is, whether his relationship with God is in order.[47]

The following viewpoints seem to me worth considering in order to bestow upon the dialogue—and indeed the kind of dialogue we are striving for—an appropriate status within pastoral care:

1. *The character of the existential openness of Christian tradition compels dialogue.* In theology today one sees reflections here and there on whether or not the Christian faith must be passed on in

a way that can never solidify into a closed tradition but, rather, is always open to existential testing through discipleship. Thus Hans-Heinrich Knipping writes,

> The truth that Jesus proclaimed and lived will prove itself only in discipleship. It will be folly and scandal in the customary ways of living. It remains to be seen who wins in truth. Thus the proclamation, the whole canon, is a colloquy of witnesses that will continue until the end of the world. The disciple, now as then, wagers with his life's decision—that is, his faith—that the truth of Christ will prove itself. This, however, is the object of dialogue in the changing historical conditions of life. Here is the starting point of a proclamation as dialogue.[48]

Martin Ohly writes,

> Finally, we have learned to understand the canon of Scripture as the fallout of a lively and exceedingly intensive dialogue. . . . The many-sided dialogue, as it encounters us in the New Testament, takes place mainly in two ways: first, in regard to the phenomenon of Jesus, and second, in regard to the consequences that follow from the phenomenon of Jesus.[49]

This, however, can only mean that even the Christian proclamation has prepared the ground for a new possibility in carrying on dialogue. Christ himself talked to people very concretely and, indeed, to particular people in particular situations. The possibilities unfolding here of giving dialogue a new foundation have as yet hardly been developed. The focus was rather on the formation of a tradition that was passed on as instruction, even though in the history of the Christian church one can find again and again starting points for new forms of dialogue.[50] Thus we can say that faith does not have the choice of whether it wants to give itself to dialogue. Only in dialogue does it survive. Only in dialogue does it remain faith. Hence faith is irrevocably called into dialogue. It comes out of dialogue and leads into dialogue (Ernst Lange).[51] Thereby we may at the same time be bringing to expression what has repeatedly been regarded as a structural change in our time: that we can no longer bind to a blind obedience, that we can no longer lead by fatherly authority, but that it is a question only of helping people, in a relationship of equality, to come of age, so that an uncertain future can lead us to the bold venture. "No I and no you alone has authority; from equal, mutual, dialogical talking and acting comes authority, comes legitimation."[52]

2. *The character of the fundamental changeability of statements of faith compels the renunciation of false authority.* It is central to the essence of Christian faith that—not in a false *theologia gloriae*—the veil of Jesus' role and authority be given up. He bases his authority on himself alone, on his own word: "But I say to you!" This results in inevitable differences of opinion, argument with the Pharisees, and dialogue with the disciples. From case to case, so to speak, Jesus has to carry out and maintain his divine Sonship.[53] There can be no doubt that the time has finally passed when the church can speak and decree with unquestioned, preordained authority. Yet this is no reason for lament but, rather, a new opportunity for dialogue:

> Dialogue marks a situation in which neither the individual Christian nor the church nor the Bible has preordained authority. Rather, the dialogue situation is handicapped when authority is asserted in the wrong place, whether in order to conceal a personal inadequacy, to postulate an outdated world view as obligatory for faith, or to declare as God's will unjust social conditions that need to be overcome. Falsely invoked authority is clerical paternalism, because it either keeps a person underage or else wishes to do so.[54]

For the practice of pastoral care this means that the pastor must actually be governed by the knowledge that he himself does not have at his disposal an answer to the other person's question but must seek and receive it together with him. Pastoral care could, therefore, be described, according to the splendid formulation of Eberhard Müller, as the divine gift of the solidarity of a common quest for truth.[55] The aim is not for the other person to be taught or convinced but, rather, for there to be genuine openness, solidarity, and readiness to listen. Of course, the authoritarian role, once banned from the dialogue, may not be allowed to reappear unintentionally when, for example, it is recommended that the leader hold back so strenuously only so that at the end of the individual parts of the dialogue he can still be allowed a certain authoritarian interpretation.[56] In the place of an inexhaustible supply of unqualified Christian answers must finally come the admission of manifold ignorance, which Dietrich Bonhoeffer called the "qualified silence."[57] An open question, an admitted helplessness—these are in no way a declaration of bankruptcy[58] but, rather, the very opportunity to make room for possible new solutions, for the work of the Holy Spirit, for the chance that out of the solidarity of human helplessness may emerge a new possibility not yet seen.

3. Interpersonal Dynamics in Dialogue

THESIS: Every dialogue is shaped by the life history and experience of the two partners, which intrude, more or less consciously, into the present situation. Psychotherapy takes account of this fact by very consciously directing attention to the phenomena of transference and countertransference. Every other kind of dialogue relationship must also reckon with the fact that it is separated from reality by transferences and thereby receives an illusory character. The better one's own expressions of countertransference can be controlled, the easier it will then be to recognize typical behavior patterns of the other person as transference and thus to break the threatening vicious circle.

Every dialogue is nestled in the encounter between two people who both bring with them their histories however constituted, and we can never abstract from these histories. Every dialogue is attached to an external framework, within which a role is played by both the space in which it takes place and the personal characteristics of the dialogue partners, their prejudices, sensitivities, weaknesses, and strengths. All of these things seem to play no role directly in dialogue, because only in the rarest cases are they expressed. Thus, as a rule, they remain unconscious, and we are not accustomed to devoting any attention at all to these things "in the background," or to taking note of them. Nevertheless, they are a reality that in a very decisive way contributes to the success or failure of a dialogue.

We are indebted to the psychotherapists for calling attention for the first time to this state of affairs and drawing it into their treatment technique, which also proceeds, of course, as an encounter between two people. Thus we will not be able to examine the question of interpersonal dynamics in dialogue unless we consider in a little more detail psychoanalytic technique and explain the concepts of transference and countertransference, which take into account this state of affairs. First, however, we will attempt to clarify the heart of the matter in a completely unpsychoanalytic way by means of a diagram. Such a means, of course, leads to a certain crudeness in presenting the situation, but we must accept that in the bargain.

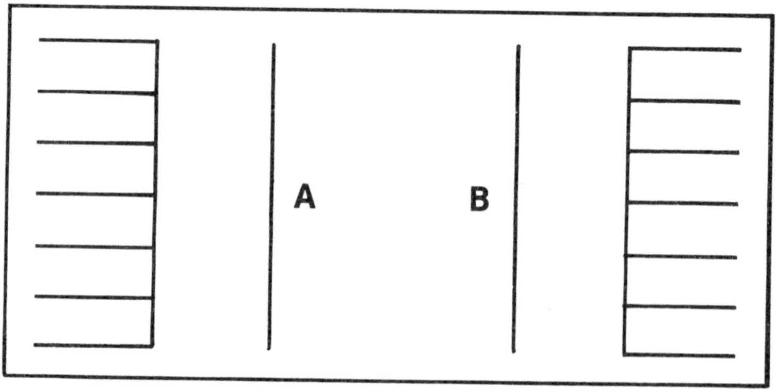

The diagram represents the two dialogue partners A and B. The line behind each of them designates the threshold of perception, which receives sense impressions and leads them further. It could also designate the boundary of consciousness beyond which lie a multiplicity of personal memories in each partner. Now, let us assume that a woman has decided to seek out a pastor because she has been advised to do so. Thus she seeks out a particular house in which the pastor meets with people. The first sense impression is evoked by this house. Let us assume that it looks familiar to her. While she is going up the steps, a thought suddenly occurs to her: This house reminds me of my old school, the one I went to as a young girl. A sudden connection is made to school days long past, and a whole stream of memories can in this way be released. Every sense impression, every perception that we have, has the aspiration of making a connection with similarly constituted memories that are stored somewhere in the great realm of our memory capacity.

Now the woman steps into the pastor's office and has a second sense impression: there is a cross hanging on the wall. Perhaps she has not been in a church in a long time, and this awakens within her a second memory: she thinks perhaps about her confirmation and everything connected with this theme. Now sitting across from her is a pastor she has never seen before, but suddenly it occurs to her that he looks like her former dance instructor. Immediately a host of memories from that time also emerge. Not a word has been spoken, the dialogue has not yet begun, but already a great wealth of previously hidden moods and feelings lie ready to express themselves and to enter the dialogue. On the side of the pastor, naturally, the situation is exactly the same.

Thus, before the dialogue is even under way, a great abundance of emotional qualities have been set in motion. Now the dialogue begins, and with each question, with each answer, with each contribution to the dialogue, the emotional situation of the two partners changes anew. There is no way to escape this, for it is a matter of a basic psychic law that is always in force. We can only close our eyes to these facts and act as if they did not exist. Then all kinds of feelings and attitudes flow into the dialogue without our being able in any way to influence or control them. Thus in our reflections it cannot be a question of how we can turn this process off. It can only be a question of how we accept these things, how we want to handle them, and how we can include them in the counseling session. For the healing dialogue, psychotherapy has developed a very specific, well-defined technique that must be regarded as fundamental for all counseling. As a rule, to be sure, the pastor lacks the prerequisites simply to adopt this technique. Yet he must be familiar with it in order to deal consciously with the phenomena of transference and countertransference. For it is precisely the transference behavior of the counselee and the pastor's expressions of countertransference that are the surest guideline for recognizing the limits of pastoral efforts. That is, the more that reality is distorted and misrepresented through expressions of transference and countertransference, the nearer lies the danger of an unallowable trespass into the realm of psychopathology.[1] Moreover, the paradigmatic experiences of psychotherapy can serve as a model for constant critical self-reflection and self-examination, which can prevent an irresponsible dilettantism and with which, therefore, every pastor should make it his duty to be familiar.

TRANSFERENCE

First, we will attempt to trace the history of psychoanalytical treatment from its beginnings until the discovery of the phenomena of transference and countertransference. The first attempts to employ dialogue as a means of therapy were undertaken at the end of the last century by the Viennese neurologist Josef Breuer. He had recognized that many patients dealt with the very unpleasant memories of certain painful experiences by pushing the memories out of their conscious minds, by repressing them. At the same time, however, the total agitation inherent in this experience was transferred into the physical body and expressed itself in symptoms of illness such as lameness, pain, and those sicknesses that today are widely regarded as psychogenic. The treatment, then, consisted in attempting to draw the agitation back out of the physical body, in order then "to compel through mental work a resolution of the contradiction between the original stimulus and the actual behavior, and through speech to eliminate the agitation."[2] Breuer called this method of treatment the cathartic method; and the healing took place, as a rule, when the patient, under hypnosis, described in the most detailed fashion possible the process that had led to the formation of his symptoms, and put into words the underlying emotional disturbance.[3]

With this method, however, Breuer achieved a completely undesired side effect, namely, that the patients began, in a characteristic way, to attach themselves to the doctor, and that this emotional attachment could be dissolved again only with great difficulty. For this reason, Breuer even hesitated to publish his research results.[4] Here already we see ourselves face to face with a principal difficulty that the pastor also meets again and again in dialogue, namely, that the dialogical situation is misrepresented and distorted by unwilled and unconscious emotional disturbances.

Freud was the first to succeed in developing firm rules and devising an art of therapeutic counseling that was equal to this situation. The rules that Freud laid down for psychoanalytical dialogue could serve as a paradigm for the unbending determination and intellectual honesty with which psychoanalysis tried, in its beginnings, to deal with these difficulties. Freud first broke with hypnosis and turned then briefly to the trick of "pressing," with which he tried, through an external sensory stimulus, to divert the patient's attention from a censorship of his thoughts and induce him to express whatever occurred to him.[5] But even this manipulation of the patient was soon abandoned, and Freud directed his complete and unrestricted attention toward the other person.

Since the patient, however, was in no position to put into words everything that actually stirred and filled him, that disturbed and tormented him, ways and means had to be found in the dialogue to read between the lines, as it were. Thus nonverbal communication was also drawn into the dialogue. Freud made it one of his rules that in an interpersonal encounter, nothing is unimportant. The other person's posture, gestures, and ways of expressing himself became speaking mirror images of his mental situation. The patient was urged to keep the dialogue intentionally without intention—that is, he was encouraged to turn himself over to random thoughts, and he was obliged by the "analytical principle" to communicate everything that came into his head, no matter whether he considered it important or unimportant, whether or not it related directly to the subject. Freud himself made "analytical abstinence" his duty. He abandoned expressing immediately his own spontaneous reactions and imparting to the patient his own judgments of taste and value. He strove instead for an attitude of "uniformly even attention" that was to be directed toward the other person with total intensity.

Freud, of course, had the same experience as his colleague

Breuer: his patients also developed inappropriate emotional attitudes toward him. Yet Freud found that these feelings could be interpreted, and he recognized in them still-virulent emotions out of the past that at that time had been directed into the unconscious and repressed and now, in the course of treatment, had been reawakened in relation to the personality of the doctor. This connection could be interpretively explained to the patient, and the supposed feelings of love or hate were dissipated. In their place came the repressed memory, the original experience. Freud now learned to understand the feelings of his patients as new editions and revisions of earlier feelings, which the patient transferred to the interpersonal situation between himself and the doctor.[6] Thereby one of the basic psychic laws became clear: Every person is subject to a compulsion to repeat. He strives to let certain important experiences that he has had with other people come to life again and to portray particular emotional attitudes of a hostile or loving nature, to act them out. Freud did not forbid this acting-out; he accepted it without going into it in a positive or negative way. He strove through interpretations, however, gradually to change this acting-out into memories, in order to work through with the patient the original experiences that were hidden behind them.[7]

What had begun as the greatest handicap in the therapeutic dialogue becomes its greatest resource. Now the dialogue no longer moves only on an intellectual plane; it includes emotional stirrings. Every part of the patient's emotional life which at first he cannot remember is experienced again in his relationship with the psychotherapist.[8] In this "increased temperature" of the transference experience, however, it is also possible to relax the symptoms. Thereby the doctor plays the role of a catalytic agent.[9] Thus the opportunity is given for a kind of reeducation. One is no longer dependent on bringing about corrections in behavior through demands but has the ready option of changing emotional attitudes through the work of interpretation.

Beginning with these basic findings, Freud gave to transference the central position in the framework of his psychoanalytic technique. Since then treatment has proceeded to a certain extent like a struggle between therapist and patient, in which the patient wants to act out, repeat, and portray his passions and feelings, while the psychoanalyst wants to compel him to submit them to thoughtful consideration.[10] How dramatic such a struggle between therapist and patient can become may be demonstrated by a brief example.

A patient who suffered from an unbearable work disorder began every therapy session by remaining silent for fifteen to twenty minutes. Over a long period of time it was never possible to bring him out of this difficulty and to help him speak openly. It took twenty to thirty hours before this resistance, which exhibited itself in silence, could be dispelled. One day, however, after he had been repeatedly asked whether he could not remember similar situations in which he had remained silent, he was able to relate, "When I came home from school and I had a failing grade and my father was waiting at the door, then I had the same feeling, for I knew, 'Now you're going to get the whip,' and then I made myself very strong and spoke not a word and locked up everything inside me."

It is astounding how, in the therapeutic situation, intellectual insight proves again and again to be powerless against the underlying emotional attitude, and how strongly the emotional attitude governs behavior. Yet as soon as it is understood that one is dealing with a transference out of the past, one generally succeeds in correcting the behavior and thereby also relaxing the symptoms.

We might ask ourselves, where is the plate made which in the course of life is regularly duplicated and printed anew? On the basis of his clinical material, Freud could only infer that the patients' need for love is not completely satisfied by reality, so that they must then turn to every new person they encounter with libidinous ideas and expectations. The doctor is set into one of these psychic series that come into being in the life of a person. The constellation of these series, however, can be shaped already by the mental images of father, mother, brother, and sister. Thus which transference the patient in psychotherapy makes depends on the peculiarity acquired during childhood years, that is, on "which love conditions he sets, which drives he satisfies, which goals he sets."[11] Transference is thus a matter of duplicating infantile imagoes—to use an expression of Jung—the dramatic highpoint of which Freud considered to be the Oedipus complex, as is well known, and which for him became the actual point of origin of transferences.[12]

Freud was of the opinion that through the constant, steady friendliness and attention of the analyst—from which he cannot allow himself to be maneuvered even by the patient's outbursts of hate or love—one could succeed in creating an intermediate state between sickness and health, an artificial illness, a pseudo-illness. In psychoanalytic technique, this intermediate state, called transference, is not at all to be warded off but rather to be resolved through analysis.[13]

There can be no question that with transference we are dealing—as Jung once expressed it—with a completely natural phenomenon that can and must be encountered by the teacher and the pastor as well as the psychotherapist.[14] We must, therefore, be clear on the point that there is no way to escape transference. On the contrary, it is the great falsifier of all our relationships. It keeps us from seeing the other person as he really is. Instead of this you, we face a ghostly shadow from the insurmountable past, which blocks our way to the real being of the other person.[15] Thus the task facing psychotherapy as well as any other counseling consists, in the first place, in turning one's attention to transference and recognizing it. But this can happen only if the pastor also has the courage to admit that much of what the counselee has expressed to him verbally and nonverbally cannot be taken at face value, that it does not immediately concern the counselor at all but comes about by way of transference or—in Jung's terminology—through projection. According to Jung, projection is an "unconscious, automatic process through which something not conscious to the subject is transferred to an object and appears to belong to that object."[16] This process occurs necessarily in every interpersonal situation.

In certain cases it will relieve the pastor if he can say, in regard to completely negative emotional reactions of the other person, that these do not concern him directly but have come about by way of projection. Perhaps this knowledge can also help avoid the panic with which so many pastoral relationships are so suddenly and unexpectedly broken off because, say, the pastor has gotten the impression that the counselee has fallen in love with him. There are extraordinarily impressive examples of this from pastoral practice.

In many cases the insight into the inevitability of transference and projection will also give rise to feelings of disappointment. What appears to the pastor perhaps as the effect of his personality or as pastoral skill, as gift or charisma, is very often revealed in this view as a very simple transference mechanism and as the pure phenomenon of projection. This recognition may often be painful, but it can also help to achieve in the dialogue an absolutely necessary inner distance and to keep the pastor and the counselee from acting out their problems together. Especially in distinctly positive or negative contacts, one must always ask oneself first whether the counselee is not placing the pastor into one of his previously practiced psychic series.

COUNTERTRANSFERENCE

Not even Freud ever asserted that when such a storm of feelings strikes the analyst, it could leave him fully unmoved. He saw clearly that with the analyst, too, there was the constant danger of an unconscious emotional attitude toward his patient, for which he coined the term countertransference. He hoped, to be sure, that the psychoanalyst—through his own analysis, which he had to undergo—could keep this countertransference to a certain extent conscious and under control. For a definition of countertransference, let us cite Fritz Riemann, who once said, "Countertransference means the psychotherapist's conscious or unconscious reactions, conditioned by his makeup or personality, to the analytical situation, the patient, his makeup, and his way of behaving in analysis."[17] To quote Freud once more,

> We have become attentive to countertransference, which arises in the doctor through the influence of the patient on the unconscious feelings of the doctor; and we are not far from raising the claim that the doctor must recognize and overcome this countertransference in himself. We have now a rather large number of persons who

> practice psychoanalysis and exchange their experiences with one another; and they have noticed that no psychoanalyst can go further than his own complexes and resistances permit. Therefore, we insist that he begin his activity with a self-analysis and continue to deepen it while he acquires his experience with patients. Whoever fails to accomplish anything in such a self-analysis may deny himself the ability to treat patients analytically.[18]

This is a clear and unambiguous position that to this day has remained the foundation for every psychoanalytical treatment.

In other dialogue situations in which this demand cannot be made, things are more complicated. First, it is a matter of sorting out to some extent the intertwining of transference and countertransference. Jung pointed above all to the fact that this intertwining of transference and countertransference in the dialogue situation frequently "creates a most awkwardly touching and unreal intimacy,"[19] which evokes resistance and doubt on both parts. For transference and countertransference produce "by means of their projection an illusionary atmosphere that either gives rise to persistent misinterpretations and misunderstandings or, conversely, simulates a downright amazing harmony, whereby the latter case is more serious than the former."[20] This possibility may arise especially when the patient is confronted with the phenomenon of guilt, for then the fact that the other person is different from oneself becomes so much more evident, and then the unconscious, as a rule, attempts to bridge the existing distance through an intensification of the attraction.[21] Thus, hidden here are the "most secret, most painful, most intensive, most tender, most shameful, most anxious, most immoral, and at the same time, the most holy feelings."[22]

Perhaps one may, in this connection, also point to a typical characteristic of this intertwining of transference and countertransference, which appears especially often in pastoral care. It concerns a phenomenon that in the language of psychotherapy is designated masochistic triumph, for the research of which we are especially indebted to American psychotherapy.[23] Let us assume that a man has learned in his relationship with his parents that only through suffering is it possible for him to dominate.

The idea that he should no longer suffer threatens the love and care coupled with his suffering. Once this attitude is acquired, it is then transferred also to other situations and thereby, in many cases, puts such a person in the position of carrying through even with the pastor his demands for love and security through suffering, through some kind of psychic or even spiritual or religious affliction that he stubbornly holds on to. Franz Heigl has pointed out that, in terms of manifestations of countertransference on the side of the psychotherapist, such an instance of transference is frequently met by a profound uneasiness that can rise to the level of anxiety.[24]

It is the pastor, above all, who seems to be especially in danger of falling victim to such countertransference anxiety. He will then try to counter either with friendly persuasion or attempts at pacification, or see himself called to redouble his efforts, which will often overstep the limits and boundaries set for the pastoral relationship. The only outcome of these well-intentioned efforts will be that the unconscious of the counselee will be spurred on to ever-greater demands and will always celebrate far-reaching masochistic triumphs. Then, after a period of intensive effort, the pastor often does not know how else to help himself except by abruptly breaking off the relationship. The counselee has once more experienced the parent-child relationship and fallen into deep resignation: "That's just the way people are—even those in the church." Such an experience of disappointment will lead him ever deeper into the despair that finally bars the entrance to the world of faith, in which he perhaps could have found help. Our good hearts and our willingness to help are not enough here. Many times we let ourselves be tempted by our good-heartedness and what we call love to do things that we are not equal to. It would be better here to see our own limits and not fall victim to a willingness to help that overextends itself.

INTERPERSONAL DYNAMICS IN THE PASTORAL DIALOGUE

Let us now turn to the question of how to deal with the phenomena of transference and countertransference in the pastoral dialogue. Even if the pastor could consider himself basically on equal ground with the psychotherapist in regard to the task of recognizing transference and countertransference and taking them into consideration during the course of the counseling process, he would still lack the prerequisites for achieving a technically elegant application of his knowledge. He is in a much more difficult situation than that of the psychotherapist. For the latter, psychotherapeutic technique, which he must master before going into practice, offers a relatively unambiguous methodology. He can wait peacefully and calmly, maintaining analytical abstinence, until the transference blossoms to full flower. For such a development he frequently has at his disposal fifty to a hundred therapy sessions. On the basis of his training and experience, he can then, as a rule, perceive the true significance of the transference and interpret it step by step to the patient. To the extent that the patient understands these transference phenomena and accepts their interpretation, they dissipate by themselves; their illusionary character becomes apparent. On the basis of his own analysis during training and the continuing, unending analysis of his personality, the psychotherapist can oversee and control his own manifestations of countertransference.

The pastor, on the other hand, finds himself in a completely different situation. He has no clear technique at his disposal. As a rule, he has behind him no analysis of his own personality to provide aid. By the nature of things, the path that psychotherapy takes is blocked for him. Also, as far as I can see, there has been no intensive discussion of this phenomenon in the literature. A few new textbooks point to the fact but offer no satisfactory solution to the problems posed. As correct as is the demand occasionally raised in this connection—namely, that the transference attachment made to the pastor be transformed into an attachment to God grounded in faith—so difficult is it, nevertheless, to get any detailed information on how this should happen. Here, however, it seems to me, lie the real difficulties to which in the long run we cannot close our eyes. In this connection, solutions and prescriptions cannot be offered. We can only give a few guidelines that perhaps contain possibilities of solutions.

We have seen that we cannot escape the dynamic interplay of transference and countertransference. In every dialogue relationship, transference is also needed. We need a certain amount of emotional relationship between the pastor and the counselee if the dialogue is not to remain on a fully abstract, intellectually narrowed level. Yet one could attempt not to reinforce the transference phenomena unnecessarily, that is, try to keep them at a level appropriate to the pastoral situation. To that end, several points can be mentioned. The more points of attachment we offer for a transference, the more strongly it will develop. The more strongly we present right from the beginning our own preferences, value judgments, and personal attitudes, the more points of contact the counselee will find for his unconscious psychic needs. In this regard, it does not matter, basically, whether the transference is the positive or the negative kind. Even in a transference relationship with an expressly negative tone something can be initiated and undertaken in the course of a pastoral relationship. It need not lead absolutely to a breaking-off of the dialogue.

The great difficulty for the pastor seems to me to be that he has a double function to exercise. On the one side, he must be the partner of the counselee, but on the other side, he must also be the representative of reality. If I am only the partner of another person, then the counselee will perhaps have an intense experience of community, a wonderful emotional attachment, a beautiful relationship. We must, however, be clear on the point that this relationship can never be exactly what the counselee wants and what he would like to make of it. He would like to bring into complete congruence his unconscious need and what the pastor places at his disposal in the partnership. The more infantile and disturbed he is, the more far-reaching will be his wants in this regard. The want inundates reality and can increase to the point where it is unfulfillable. The pastor cannot offer him what he wants, for the pastor is, of course, not his father, his brother, his sister, or his lover. The pastor is rather the representative of the reality in which this person stands, with which he must come to terms, and to which he must return after the encounter.

The pastoral task, it seems to me, moves methodologically between these two poles. We cannot offer the counselee unlimited attention but rather should make clear to him in the first session that it is a matter of a partnership of limited duration that must one day be broken off, and that the partnership that we have to offer is definitely a partial one. Thereby we bring reality into play.

Now, in pastoral care there are also, from time to time, people who attempt to increase the intensity of the attention, who want to be in closer contact, who perhaps voice a wish for a home visit, who want to talk about more intimate areas of life, or who even request common undertakings. This raises the question of the amount of attention. When one enters into a pastoral relationship that could possibly last over a long period of time, it is advantageous in every case to limit from the very beginning the length of the individual sessions. Experience shows that a standard of about 50 minutes can serve as an aid to orientation. There are pastors who boast that they have three-hour, four-hour, and even longer evening sessions. It must be doubted, however, whether in such dialogues reality continues to be represented in an adequate way.

When we attempt to mark the interpersonal dynamic of the pastoral dialogue with the two key words "partnership" and "reality," this means that one should try to bring the two positions designated by the words into a dialectical relationship with each other. As a rule, if it comes to an absolutization of the pole of partnership, we simply stimulate often infantile wants and needs. We fall into the role of an uncritical need satisfier, and such an indulging attitude usually, experience has shown, only releases ever-increasing wants, because it makes it possible for the inner life of the counselee to flee into an emotional movement backwards, a regression, that consists in a revival of the decrepit wants and longings of the past.

If the pole of reality is absolutized, the impression could arise that pastoral care is simply a matter of a similarly uncritical accommodation to the givens of one's living situation, including its social conditions. Often enough, however, we must acknowledge the basic justification of the counselee's wants, needs, and longings; that is, we must agree with him in regard to his surroundings and the social conditions under which he lives. As a rule, he lacks only the opportunity to change this, his reality, so that he can lead a dignified life. For this reason he often seeks out the pastor, and the latter's task will then be to help him realize his wants in the sense of an appropriate modification of reality. Psychoanalytic theory designates this ability the "ego function" and contrasts it with the pure satisfaction of needs, which the id wants to compel, and with the pure accommodation that the superego demands.

Such a strengthening of the critical ego function, therefore, does not mean a total renunciation of convictions of any kind on the part of the pastor. If this were the basic attitude and position, a real dialogue would seem to me no longer possible. We would then become only the echo of the ideas and opinions of the partner, and with this a dialogue sooner or later runs aground and falls apart. When someone seeks out a pastor, he does it, of course, not only with the intention of getting his own ideas set before himself again in some kind of mirror fashion. He does it, indeed, also with a readiness perhaps to accept in the bargain a correction of currently held attitudes and ideas. To be sure, such aid to orientation—which we owe to the other person and which compels us actually to have our own opinion on the basic problems of human life—is not given too hastily. It should, in any case, be inserted into the dialogue as an offer, as a recommendation, and not until we are sure that the questioning of our partner has to some extent really been understood. There is certainly a danger that we will answer too quickly the questions posed to us by the counselee. It is always more important to answer the questioner than the question, and often the importance and scope of a question cannot be recognized until the underlying problems have been revealed. Then it frequently becomes apparent that it has to be answered entirely differently from the way one would have answered it on first impulse.

The same is true in the telling of personal experiences. As a general rule, this is not very useful, for what may have helped me in a particular situation is not at all bound to help another person in another situation, even though it may be very similar. In any case, extreme discretion is in order here. Above all, however, we should seriously ask ourselves why we are inclined repeatedly to put into words particular experiences in our lives. Concealed here, perhaps, is our own unconscious need, and we are misusing the other person in order to satisfy this, our own need.

With that we come to the most decisive aspect of this whole problem. In the pastoral dialogue, practically everything can be allowed methodologically if one has clearly in mind why it is being done. Thus it is especially important that the interpersonal dynamics of such a dialogue be clarified and illuminated in regard to countertransference.

CRITICAL SELF-EXAMINATION OF THE PASTOR

It can hardly be raised as a general principle that every pastor must, by means of a thorough training analysis, become master of all his possible countertransference manifestations. Nonetheless, the requirement remains that he control them to some degree. The psychotherapist cannot carry out psychotherapeutic treatment unless he has first experienced such treatment of his own person. Those who are put into a counseling situation have first experienced a kind of training counseling, counseling of one's own person; and here and there the demand has been made that pastoral counseling be practiced only by those who themselves are in a pastoral counseling relationship. This raises an extremely difficult requirement, but one can scarcely get away from the principle that an optimum of creative activity is reached only when there is also an opportunity for fruitful self-evaluation. At this point, the traditional structure of a minister's position offers him rather few possibilities. He should, however, take cognizance of the fact that it can be an extraordinarily great help in pastoral counseling if he has succeeded in bringing clarification to the shadowy regions of his own life to the extent that they do not force themselves obtrusively into pastoral or counseling relationships. This certainly does not mean anything like moral perfection or a striving for superiority. We must, however, be clear on the point that we misuse the dialogue situation when, under the pretext of helping, we exploit it for the satisfaction of our own unfulfilled desires and longings and thereby make the counselee the object of wants and needs, however subtle.

For those working in an institutional counseling position, teamwork offers the greatest help. For the pastor, however, it is especially hard for teamwork to get established, because it also includes a willingness for critical self-examination in a group, and we can agree to that only with great difficulty. The best suited for pastoral care is surely the person who has learned how to solve life's problems without the living lies of repression. On the way to repression one can often succeed in achieving an impeccable life style according to moral standards. But all the unacceptable desires and stirrings that have been banned from consciousness and now lead a sinister shadow existence in the unconscious are only lying in wait to unload themselves and can lead to precipitate actions when the powers of the unconscious are required in an encounter. Yet every interpersonal situation in dialogue requires the powers of the unconscious. Therefore the demand must be made that after every dialogue one confess to oneself with radical honesty even painful and reprehensible impulses, instead of repressing them. For it is a fact of psychological experience that the strength of desires and drives that are not allowed by the conscious mind is in no way diminished if they are banned from consciousness; on the contrary, it increases and forms a dangerous, emotionally explosive force in the unconscious. Thus, in this situation also, Jung's statement applies, that one "must give to consciousness that attitude which allows the unconscious to cooperate instead of opposing."[25]

Hence, what resources are there for achieving such an attitude? In what follows, I shall attempt to define, at least by way of suggestion, the direction in which one might find a critical self-examination in the form of some questions about one's own motivation. Anyone who enters into personal counseling should regularly ask himself such questions in order thus to initiate an ongoing process, which should lead, preferably, to regular monitoring sessions with a colleague, that is, a kind of supervision; or they can be discussed in a group setting, as is done under the aegis of clinical pastoral education or continuing education in pastoral psychology. Needless to say, these questions should not be misunderstood moralistically as schematic stereotypes or even in the sense of a magazine quiz. They can indicate only one direction:

What expectations do I harbor in regard to the counselee? A great deal is said today about the fact that there is an occupational illness among people in social work, and that the name of this occupational illness is embitterment. It is very easy, indeed, to see how a person can become embittered when he spends his whole life in a vocation in which he repeatedly experiences disappointments because his well-intentioned attempts to help people continually run aground. And how he is to deal with this situation is a question of psychic hygiene. It is wholly apparent that in response to the question, What do I expect from the counselee? the desire to help must first supply the motive for every pastoral dialogue. But along with this desire could there not also be expectations indicating that this giving of help is supposed to compensate us for so much that we otherwise must do without in life, that those dialogues—which often are also extremely satisfying—are supposed to compensate us for all that remains unfulfilled in our life? Here we must ask ourselves if we are in a position really to be able, in the long run, to endure and work through the disappointing experiences that every dialogue necessarily brings with it. For with the occupational illness of embitterment comes a skepticism vis-à-vis other people that no longer lets us expect anything positive. If we again bring to mind the circular structure of every dialogue, it will become clear that this unconscious skepticism of the pastor is also transferred to the counselee. That is, the actual result—especially in a dialogue relationship lasting over a longer period of time—is communication between the unconscious minds of both partners, and we experience again and again the surprising fact that the expectations we bring to another person actually influence his behavior.

Why must I make myself indispensable? This question points to the danger of an insistent willingness to help, which is found everywhere and in all vocations, but above all in the pastor. For he is under an especially strong obligation to relieve the counselee, who comes to him with a certain helplessness, of what that person could perhaps do for himself. Whoever enjoys in a special way the gratitude of people who come to him in their need should ask himself whether or not he must satisfy an especially strong, unsatisfied need for attention coming from his own childhood, so that he exploits current dialogue situations to compensate for this lack.

In what area am I especially inclined toward repression? In our society we are still in a process of transition in attitudes toward sexuality. When one examines the writing in pastoral-care texts of a century ago, in which the pastor's attention is drawn to the kinds of shocking abominations he will see and hear among the people, one sees clearly the self-evidence with which it is presupposed that he himself, the reverend pastor, is completely free from these abominations. Even today there is still among us that attitude of absolute certainty which is so sure that the reprehensible drives observed in others do not exist at all in ourselves, do not even lie in the realm of possibility, play absolutely no role, and therefore are completely beyond consideration. Even if we have come to a more realistic view in regard to the area of sexuality, it seems to me that the change in this attitude is still very incomplete in regard to the area, say, of aggression; and we must still work through very many unconscious areas of our own spiritual makeup.

Do we have a need to adopt a special defensive stance vis-à-vis homosexuality? Human beings are bisexually constituted psychically as well as physically. We all carry within us both sexual possibilities in rudimentary form. It is the special task of childhood, youth, and maturity to become accustomed to the role of the man and the role of the woman. During the process the sexually opposite portions of our personality always remain present. They are simply pushed, for the most part, into the unconscious. The necessity for an especially strong defense against this area can, of course, also intrude very disruptively into the counseling relationship. Until now, this aspect has received no attention at all. To be sure, it is admitted that distortions and displacements through sexuality can come between a man and a woman in a pastoral dialogue, but no one ever considers the possibility that this may also happen between partners of the same sex. There are very subtle forms of homoerotic possibilities of encounter and relationship, and they are presented to us more often than we expect by counselees. We should therefore consciously come to terms with them. To that end, we must also to some extent know and become conscious of our own feelings in this direction.

Why must I always be so nice to everyone? Precisely in the counseling situation there is again and again the obligation that everything here move in a way that is as friendly, loving, and fatherly or motherly as possible. If the pastor cannot permit himself to break off the counseling session when the time has come, or to take a position when it is needed, then the assumption lies close at hand that his inability to say no is connected with unresolved feelings of guilt. They can keep us from being able to maintain properly a consistent attitude and force us continually to try to adapt ourselves and oblige the counselee. His expectations become so powerful a criterion that we dare not make him angry, for fear that we will lose him and he will withdraw from us his favor.

Why am I actually so legalistic in my dialogues? We will also, of course, have the exactly opposite problem from that of the previous question; that is, the dialogue will come to certain points where we think that here we must now say clearly and firmly what is right and wrong and, so to speak, box the counselee's ears with the lawbook. We would do well here to ask ourselves a question about our own unresolved aggression. Every legalistic element in counseling hides a bit of aggression, which, however, is concealed and masked according to the structure of our personality.

Why do I feel myself drawn so strongly toward the spiritually weaker person? In pastoral counseling we must take into account the fact that we deal with people who are spiritually weak, who cannot cope with their lives on their own. Here arises the unexpectedly great possibility of dominating through helping. This presents an opportunity that is very often seized. Those who have few other possibilities of assuaging yearnings for power are the very ones who must guard themselves against seeking out particularly the spiritually weaker person as a partner.

Why do I find other people so interesting? It may be one of the motives of the pastoral vocation that one finds people so immensely interesting that one is fascinated with the idea of always having people in front of one, of always facing the task of getting inside a person and understanding him. It may sound a little misguided if one also seeks to trace this exploring urge to its roots in early childhood, but it can be demonstrated without doubt that a very strong, unconscious motive for a person's directing his urge to explore toward other people lies in the fact that he himself in his early childhood was hindered in his sexual explorations. There are cases in the psychoanalysis of young theology students in which this motive unconsciously determined entirely the choice of vocation.

With the foregoing questions we have attempted to bring a few typical basic attitudes under the scrutiny of a critical self-examination, so that they will not play an unconscious and unrecognized role in the interpersonal dynamics of dialogue. When, in the following section, we describe from practical experience some of the typical modes of behavior of the counselee, it is not at all with the intention of structuring some kind of typology but to show how much the previous experiences of a counselee shape his behavior. Observation of transference-conditioned behavior thus becomes the surest way to arrange and provide a basis for our assumptions about possible corrective measures.

SOME TYPICAL MODES OF BEHAVIOR AS INDICATORS OF INTERPERSONAL DYNAMICS IN DIALOGUE (CASE STUDIES)

Provocation. A young man appeared for counseling and immediately attempted to involve the counselor in his struggle for his rights. He found himself at great odds with his superiors. In a whole series of different positions he had had difficulties with his superiors, who, as a result, finally got the impression that there was something wrong with him. Pedagogically, it was certainly very unwise to instruct him that he might want to seek out a counselor. He came already somewhat under protest and tried to expound to the counselor why he was in the right and all his superiors were in the wrong. The first critical point of such counseling consists in the danger of going into the problem in such a way that one allows oneself to be pushed to one side or the other. Both possibilities are wrong. At first it is a question, rather, of showing interest in the counselee and his life history and making it clear to him that one is interested in the counselee himself. When this happened in the case just described, the behavior of the counselee changed. He tried to push the counselor into the role of an authoritarian psychological dogmatician. He had read a few books on psychology and psychoanalysis, and from that he projected psychological judgments onto the counselor. In this process, absolutely no psychological word was said, but the young man was under a certain psychic compulsion to prove to his counselor that he was mistaken. When this also proved unsuccessful and the counselor, during several sessions, did not allow himself to be maneuvered away from a steady level of attention and friendliness, the counselee became unpunctual, did not come at all for some sessions, or appeared at a time other than the appointed one, and caused thereby a series of difficulties that all seemed to be aimed at provoking the counselor to reject him or condemn him.

A closer analysis of this curious behavior shows that it had little to do with the counselor but was, rather, to be deemed the result of a father-transference. His father had been a Nazi and after the collapse in 1945 had been dismissed from his position. A few years later he had died, but for the rest of his life he had devoted himself exclusively to fighting for his supposed "right." Superficially, the son had disassociated himself from his father's views on life, but unconsciously he had identified with his father and thus tried to continue waging his father's battle against the whole world. Later, behind the father-identification, a tendency toward revenge against his father also became clear. The latter had been a stern, very domineering man who had walked around only in military boots and with his cold-hearted nature had caused his son endless suffering. Had the counselor accepted the challenge that the counselee had presented to him by dealing prematurely with the problem in the foreground, he might, presumably, never have got to this man's actual need.

Manipulation of the counselor. Negative transference can go so far that the counselor is lured into certain measures that then allow a negative counterreaction by the counselee. A young husband showed a thoroughly negative attitude toward the counselor. He continually passed negative judgments; the counselor never got a smile from him, never a look of agreement; it was always like facing a wall. He was plagued by a great jealousy of his young wife, who worked in an office where she had two young men as bosses. Every little sign of friendliness or courtesy toward his wife from one of these bosses made the man sick with jealousy. Suddenly he made to the counselor the surprising proposal that he might want to call the wife into the office, since he had the impression that she should be heard too. One of the central difficulties of this marriage consisted in the fact that before the wedding the couple had enjoyed very satisfying sexual contacts with each other, but with the wedding these had come to an end and considerable sexual troubles had arisen. On the part of the man, they were evidenced by impotence; for the woman sexual intercourse suddenly caused very great pain. Now, when the request of the counselee also to call in his wife was not granted but he was asked instead to tell what occurred to him, what he imagined, what he hoped for in making such a request, he confessed, after great embarrassment, the following revealing fantasy: His wife is in the office for counseling. He comes rushing up from outside. He finds the door locked, kicks it in with his feet, and surprises the counselor in an awkward position with his wife, whereupon without a word he strikes him down. It would certainly have been a mistake to comply with the wish to involve the wife in the counseling. The newly created situation would have served as a pretext for letting an unbearable aggression burst forth. In the background lay the memory of a truly fearsome father, who was a drinker, was constantly beating the mother, and with his monstrous brutality had tyrannized the whole family.

Attempts at solidarity. There are counseling cases in which the counselee, if he has come to a counselor of the same sex, is at pains to establish something like a solidarity between comrades of the same gender. Thus an older man who came with the intention of getting divorced continually used the line: "Oh, you know; we're both men here." In this case it came to light after a while that his will to divorce could not be realized, because he still identified with his very strict, tradition-conscious father. His attempt to find solidarity with the counselor must be regarded as an effort to bring about a relaxation of the strongly ingrained authority of his conscience. He found himself in an unusually serious dilemma because he had already created a new situation in regard to his marriage. He lived only half the week with his family, a wife seven years older and three almost-grown daughters, while he spent the other half of the week with his mistress, who was twenty years younger. He had bought her a small house on the edge of the city, and she had already borne him two sons. This man's real problem must be seen in his inability to make responsible decisions. It would certainly not be remedied by the satisfaction of his desires for solidarity. In a similar way, the often decisively expressed wish of many wives only to be counseled by a "more mature woman"—with whom they then seem to feel at home, above all in complaining about the world of men in general—can arrest and delay any genuine progress in understanding.

Flight into contact. In the work of counseling there are also energetic people who establish contact very easily, of whom one quickly gets the impression that they really have both feet on the ground, that they have things under control and are soon ready to speak openly. Often, however, it becomes apparent after a time that the contact is only of a very superficial nature and without any depth. One such counseling case even involved an encounter-group professional, a man who held a traveling position within the church and went from conference to conference to give lectures on love and marriage, while his lonely wife, with an immense feeling of being left all by herself, was near suicide. In counseling, this joy of contact without depth was very much in the forefront of the man's behavior. As soon as this was used as a model for the rest of his behavior, something very interesting came to light. In his youth this man had had a large number of acquaintances with girls which all progressed to a certain point while retaining a certain lack of commitment, and then were broken off almost in a panic. But then he fell into the hands of a girl who seized on the firm resolve to marry him and who also carried out this intention. With this, however, the troubles began, because he was now forced out of his noncommittal approach to contact and had to give himself to another person. He avoided this, however, by taking up his traveling activity, which did not allow his wife to take part in his life. Thus he tried to overcome his fear of profound contact by persistently evading a responsible relationship with his wife. Now he faced the question of getting a divorce, since he had met another girl, with whom he had no sexual relationship at all but with whom he believed he could live together. In this case, his behavior in counseling could be used to make him understand how much he was under a compulsion toward repetition, and that with a new partner he would find himself, in two or three years at the most, in exactly the same situation he was in now.

Interest in the question of guilt. It is especially in marital counseling that we meet both husbands and wives whose politeness is exemplary, who immediately gain our favor, and who awaken with their arguments the impression that they are completely in the right. With one husband of this type it occurred to the counselor that one thing seemed to be missing, namely, the emergence of any kind of emotion. He presented his problems as if it were a matter of a scientific experiment and described his wife like some strange kind of insect that had nothing to do with his life. He actually showed interest only in his own posture of fairness and integrity in regard to his wife, who represented a completely different type. He had actually come for counseling only for the purpose of having it confirmed that his judgment in the matter was correct. Thus many people have a burning interest in bringing up the question of guilt at the beginning of the counseling sessions in the hope of presenting everything in such a way that the other, the absent, partner will receive the guilt. This interest in going into the question of guilt at the start of marital counseling should be met head on, even to the point of asserting, "For the moment the question of guilt does not interest me at all; instead, we should first attempt to understand what actually goes on in your marriage and how you get along with each other." As soon as this is tried, the situation is often shown in a completely different light, and one sees that even behind fairness and objectivity can be entirely different problems, which would probably never come into view if one accepted the initial posture.

Demonstrative suffering. There are people who give the impression that they tell their tale of suffering—which, objectively viewed, can actually be a horror story—only so that they can feed on it. One has the feeling that they really live on their suffering and also on being able to portray this suffering. In one case a woman in counseling told of very serious bodily symptoms, which finally led to terminal cancer. On the outside, the marriage seemed to be completely normal, but the man fled into his work because he simply could no longer bear his wife's passionate willingness to suffer and almost fanatical will to suffer. Here one is in danger of falling into an attitude of pity and also of giving clear expression to this pity. Nothing, however, is gained thereby, but on the contrary, many opportunities that we might have with such a person are precluded. For the counselee can already manipulate these situations effortlessly. He has learned, namely, to use suffering to make an impression and through suffering to compel from other people certain particular reactions. Interpersonal relations are thereby reduced to pity, and all other reciprocal encounters and genuine possibilities for dialogue are excluded. Therefore, the more objectively we respond to such behavior and the less we let ourselves be drawn into explicit expressions of pity, the greater is the opportunity, in solidarity and partnership, of opening up possible life styles other than simply the described willingness to suffer.

Infantilism. A person comes in for counseling who immediately begins to cry and initiates the relationship with outbreaks of despair in which the repeated refrain is, "Please, tell me what I should do. I will do anything. Just tell me what I need to do." Such psychic instability often does not allow any kind of intellectual commonality in the accomplishments of life; there is simply a gigantic need to regain an authority figure that somehow got lost along life's way. Frequently, such a person has already married a father or mother figure and is now attempting to push the same role onto the counselor: he is supposed to become the one who gives instructions—which then, naturally, are not carried out—who issues clear prohibitions, and who takes measures. Often infantilism can go so far that only psychotherapeutic treatment can help. In pastoral care and counseling, efforts in behalf of an infantile person will take a long time, in which we must try, with a certain relentlessness, to get this person to take small steps for himself. We should relieve him of nothing, do nothing for him, except repeatedly help him to understand his situation and its pressure toward regression. We can stimulate in him a desire for independent reflection and illumination of his problematic situation so that he will then take in hand the things he can and must do for himself.

Passive submissiveness. A little different from infantilism is the behavior of the person who immediately opens the dialogue with the remark, "I know, of course, that everything is my fault. I did everything wrong, you see, and now I would like to know from you how I can do it differently. I'm completely ready; just tell me the points at which I have to change. Then I'll turn everything around; I'll rebuild myself from the ground up and demonstrate a completely different kind of behavior." Here we could have a case of what psychoanalysts, in researching the manifestations of basic drives, call the complete reversal. Frequently, the person involved has basically unrelenting demands for power. In the course of his life, however, he has learned that, displayed so openly, these demands do not pay, that one comes off much better if one tries to conceal them, push them aside, and replace them with a passive-submissive attitude. With such passive-submissive people it can be really fruitful to seek out and research, almost like a detective, where in the counselee's life history and everyday living situation his original attitude is concealed and yet perhaps expresses itself. It may be present in every case if we only listen attentively and try attentively to see the way things are.

This description of behavior during counseling could certainly be continued to any length. The point to be made is that the behavior of the counselee in the dialogue situation can itself very often be the key to the difficulties that have actually brought this person to us but which he himself cannot yet name. When duly observed, transference can be a very substantial means of helping the counselee perceive what he just cannot describe. He gives, instead, one thing and another that we must regard as rationalizations, for some kind of rational basis can always be found and must then be offered to conceal the real reasons. Even in the least cases, the counselees can give us no definite reasons why things are this way and not that. It seems to be one of the basic needs of human beings to rationalize and repeatedly put forth excuses and reasons. We would let ourselves be duped if we were to go into these reasons, if we were to take them at face value and let them be our only source of information. But the behavior with which a person approaches us, what demands he makes of us, the picture that comes together out of the many individual observations made during counseling—all of this can serve as a model for other living situations, such as the way he treats his wife and how he approaches his children. Therefore, here again we must express the admonition to be very reserved with one's own reactions at the beginning of the dialogue, in order first to be able to observe how the counselee behaves toward the counselor, what transference he makes, into which role he tries to maneuver the counselor. Only when I can see the total picture, more or less, will I be able gradually to come out of my reserve, because only then will a controlled counseling session be possible.

4. Means and Methods in Counseling

THESIS: Among the most important means of conducting counseling are a basic attitude that establishes and promotes relationship, an adequate understanding of verbal and nonverbal communication, a knowledge of the regularity of the question-and-answer process, and the earnest will to recognize and avoid any suggestiveness as the great threat to the character of the dialogue. The theological principle of freedom provides the criteria that can help one become oriented in the face of methodological pluralism in the field of counseling.

The special difficulty of an elegant methodology of counseling lies in the fact that in this field only limited objective assertions can be made. When we name a certain attitude and approach as the most important means of conducting counseling, then that may be disappointing for many, because it is evident that such an attitude cannot be learned and adopted without effort. Nonetheless, the requirement of a particular basic attitude is supposed to make it understood that anyone who goes into counseling must find himself constantly and repeatedly under the obligation to examine and clarify his own outlook. Only then will he succeed in finding the understanding that must be regarded as a further, most important prerequisite for conducting dialogue. Especially in shorter dialogues, it will be essentially a matter of understanding and assimilating the often well-hidden and enciphered code value of certain communications and remarks.[1] Relatively speaking, the clearest and most unambiguous area of counseling can be indicated by what empirical psychology has worked out and set forth under the caption of the question-and-answer process, including here, above all, the interview technique. With such a clear methodology, we must, nevertheless, not lose sight of the fact that the actual goal of pastoral counseling is the free and new experience of our partner, and that therefore, faced today with the various counseling methods that have already been developed, we can only orient ourselves with a methodology that can serve this goal.

PROMOTING RELATIONSHIP

An attitude is difficult to describe; it can more easily be developed interpretively in retrospect from a particular mode of behavior. Therefore, in the following pages are two dialogues that Ruth Bang presents in her book *Hilfe zur Selbsthilfe* (Help for self-help) and through which we can best make clear the difference between a basic attitude that impedes and one that promotes relationship.[2]

> *Social worker, Miss A. (very interested and friendly, after a short, obliging greeting, to which Jenny in no way responds; she is instead very much "buttoned up"; for a second she casts a distrustful and rather negative look toward the social worker):* I'm sure you can imagine, Jenny, why I have asked you to come and see me.
>
> *Jenny (shrugs her shoulders, then a little later, rather explosively):* No, why did you, really?
>
> *Miss A. (a little astonished and somewhat tense, but controlled and not unfriendly):* Do you actually mean, Jenny, that everything is all right with you? Couldn't you very well use some advice and help?
>
> *Jenny (stubborn and withdrawn, speaking through her teeth and barely understandable):* I wouldn't know, why?
>
> *Miss A.:* Well, then, I must tell you why we have asked you to come in: it has been reported to us that you may be expecting a child.
>
> *Jenny (after brief reflection, bristling up and arrogant):* Well, even if that were really true, what's it got to do with the Youth Office?
>
> *Miss A. (not completely free of an undertone of gentle reproach):* We believe that it's of some concern to the Youth Office whether or not a seventeen-year-old, unmarried girl gets pregnant. *(Pause.)* You are also supposed to have said that you want to jump in the river if this is the case. That sounds as if you could not deal with the whole thing so well alone after all.

Jenny (full of anger and pent-up aggression): Not that too! I wonder who's been gossiping again.

Miss A.: Jenny, I think you should be a little more reasonable and discuss the matter with me completely openly, so that we can find out how we can help you.

Jenny (lowers her head; tears come to her eyes; it is not clear whether from worry, defiance, or rage): Well, what else is left for me to do? Just what can there be to discuss? Talking won't make the baby go away again, either.

Miss A. (mildly indignant at the insolent tone): No, of course not.

Jenny: Well, then, I'll find out myself how I'm going to deal with it.

Miss A.: By jumping into the river? Don't you know, that would be a great injustice—against the baby, too? I believe there might be better ways to straighten out what you have done. We can all make mistakes, but then we must also have the courage to correct our errors. Don't you think so, too?

Jenny (sullen and hostile): But where can I go? My parents have said that if I got pregnant, I should arrange to get out of the house as soon as possible, so that I would not disgrace them any more in front of the whole neighborhood. They are furious with me and won't say a word to me.

Miss A.: Your parents are probably very disappointed with you. Still, it's understandable, actually, that they are angry. You would have to understand that, too. *(Pause.)* Do you know whether you are pregnant?

Jenny (stubbornly silent, then): I just can't go on anymore! Especially when it's not my fault at all!

Miss A. (not without mild indignation, which she controls with effort): Now, wait just a minute! You're trying to make the whole thing a little too easy. I want to tell you something, Jenny. Now, just try to talk with me reasonably and openly about the whole affair. Then we'll see what's to be done.

Jenny shrugs her shoulders again defiantly, presses her lips together, and persistently pulls on her handkerchief, as if she wants to tear it up. In the course of the dialogue, Miss A. has become a little insecure, because Jenny is so unapproachable and obstinate. Her insecurity also awakens in her impatience and exasperation. She thinks, therefore, that it would be good, in any case, to point out to Jenny the possible ways in which an agency might be able to give practical help in such a situation. She also asks whether Jenny is working regularly in her apprentice position, which Jenny affirms. And then . . .

Miss A.: What would you think of my talking with your parents?

Jenny (literally bursts out): For God's sake, not that too! If they knew that I was in the Youth Office! I was sure glad that I was able to intercept your letter.

Miss A.: Jenny, I don't think we're going to get very far this way. Ultimately, I can't put everything in order again for you if you don't help me with it. In the end, however, you are the one who made your bed, and you will have to lie in it. But now you know that you can get help with it and that you have no reason to despair. Remember that it concerns not only you but also the child. *(Faced with the stubborn girl, she mentally gathers herself together and proceeds in as friendly a manner as possible.)* I recommend that you calmly reflect once again on everything I have said to you and then come to me again. Perhaps a week from today?

Jenny: Well, if you say so. *(When the social worker offers her a parting handshake, she makes a kind of curtsying movement and grumbles something like:)* Goodbye!

Looking at this dialogue, one can see clearly why a basic attitude that establishes relationship cannot be presupposed here and why the dialogue must, with logical consistency, lead to a fiasco. The following points are perhaps important:

1. The opening of the dialogue already presupposes an understanding which, at best, the dialogue itself could evoke but which can never be made the presupposition of a dialogue that has come about under a special handicap: the client has come not voluntarily with a particular concern but on command. Such a dialogue can, therefore, never be opened with the stock expression "I'm sure you can imagine why you had to come in."

2. Already as the second reaction to the defensive and denying attitude of the dialogue partner, there follows a moral reproach that accosts the partner with the word that not everything in her life is in order.

3. In reaction to her defiance and negative attitude, a reciprocal negative mental state breaks through, which expresses itself as reproach and disparagement and declaration of the partner's incompetence, and which forcefully—almost as if with a blow from a club—brings to expression the central problem for the sake of which this dialogue is being held.

4. Even though the counselor's own indignation can only be controlled with effort, she makes a demand for radical openness,

which, naturally, can never come by way of a demand but must always be a free gift of the partner.

5. The agreement-seeking question "Don't you think so, too?" is brought into play at a point where it cannot be used in any case, for understanding has already been seriously disturbed by the previous course of the dialogue. Both partners have moved far apart from each other.

6. The social worker does not see herself primarily as the client's partner but rather shows the client that she intends herself to be understood as a spokesperson and advocate for what the girl feels to be the hostile world around them. In this way she drives the girl further into resistance.

7. Now the attempt is made to outmaneuver the clearly shown resistance of the dialogue partner through an imperative to openness, which therefore leads, logically, to greater resistance.

8. Because she is helpless to make a concrete offer, the social worker apparently falls into a panic and goes over completely into the enemy camp. The offer to speak to the parents is felt simply as betrayal; it must make the dialogue partner fear that everyone is coming down on her at once, and it drives her into complete isolation.

9. Thus the outcome is necessarily the paniclike breaking off of dialogue by the social worker.

In the practice of pastoral care, there are more than a few dialogues that, at least in the occasion and the problem, are similar to the preceding one. Thus it could be instructive to visualize whether there is also another possibility—through a different basic attitude—of establishing a true relationship. Consider, therefore, the following, second dialogue:

In her outward demeanor, Jenny brings to expression the same inner attitude as in the preceding dialogue.

Miss B.: Have you wondered, Jenny, why we wrote you and asked you to come see us?

Jenny (grumpily): Yeah, naturally! So, what do you want from me?

Miss B.: Then, it's good of you to come anyway. I hope the time of our appointment was O.K. with you. You work, don't you?

Jenny: Yes.

Miss B.: Do you like your work?

Jenny: Oh, yeah!

Miss B.: And I would like to tell you why the Youth Office has asked you to come in. We are here, you see, to be concerned about people who, we must assume, find themselves in a somewhat difficult situation in life.

Jenny (somewhat irritated by the very warmhearted tone of the social worker's voice): But there's nothing wrong with me.

Miss B.: You know, it sometimes happens that other people take more interest in us than we realize, perhaps even more than we like. And so it also happens that word has reached us that you are probably expecting a baby and have said that you were going to jump in the river. Hence, we thought you could ultimately use someone like us social workers, to whom such situations are not completely foreign and with whom you could express yourself and get counseling. If you really believe it is possible that you are in a family way, then you really must, indeed, have all kinds of worries, I would think—to begin with, just from the uncertainty.

Jenny: I wonder who's been gossiping again! That's the last thing I needed! And even if it were true, what could *you* do about it? Nobody can help anybody with that.

Miss B.: Listen, Jenny. When someone gets a big scare through some bad news, then they often believe that there is no way out, and they don't see at all how they're supposed to keep going. Many times it's enough just to sleep on it, but sometimes that doesn't help either, and then you need someone who knows what to do, someone with whom you can just talk it out.

Jenny (doubtful, but somewhat "thawed"): With a total stranger?

Miss B.: You're right, Jenny. And, therefore, it wouldn't be a bad idea, perhaps, if we got to know each other a little better. You see, I don't know you at all either, and can well understand that you might not want to pour out your whole heart right away. Nor is that even necessary. But please think about it a minute and see if you can tell me something about why you believe there is apparently no way out for you.

Jenny: Well, then, where am I supposed to go? When my parents found out that I was with Harold more than once in my room, they immediately said: "What shame if you get pregnant! Then you can just find yourself a place to stay. The disgrace is unimaginable!" They are furious with me and won't say a word to me. Now, do you see that there's nothing I can do? And besides, it's not my fault that everything has happened this way.

Miss B.: Jenny, for the time being, we don't want to think at all about whether it's your fault or not. What's important is that you not believe it's all over now. Anyone who believes that must be very unhappy, and when one is unhappy, one seldom gets sensible ideas.

Jenny: My parents say my life is wrecked once and for all. *(Pause.)* Now everybody is against me.

Miss B.: And, therefore, it's your opinion that the Youth Office and the social workers are against you too.

Jenny: Well, why not?

Miss B.: That's not quite right! The Youth Office and the social workers are here to help and not to scold.

Jenny: But how do you want to help me, then?

Miss B.: Now, I can't tell you that exactly yet. I only know from experience that actually some way can always be found through calm, mutual reflection. First of all, I still know too little about you; I don't even know yet where the real problem actually is. To begin with, you must get the feeling for the first time that we here are not against you and that you don't need to be against us. After your earlier experiences, certainly, you may not believe that yet, because you assume that everybody would be angry with you if they knew what is, perhaps, your problem.

Jenny: What do you mean, "perhaps"? I'm going to have a baby. And talking won't make it go away, either.

Miss B.: That's true. And because you're expecting a baby, you believe a happy life has now passed you by?

Jenny: Well, of course!

Miss B.: I don't believe you have the right idea of what a Youth Office and a social worker are.

Jenny: To tell the truth, no! I imagined this place as something else entirely.

Miss B.: How was that?

Jenny: I thought people came here who needed money or *(hesitatingly)* who had done something and had to go into a youth home.

Miss B. (laughing): You know, your idea is not that far off. It does happen that because of illness or unemployment or for some other reason, there's not enough money in a family. Then, at times an agency can help and make sure there is enough to eat or enough heat. And, as far as the youth home is concerned, you're partially right about that too. It can happen, for example, that children don't have a beautiful home life and we must assume that they would be happier in an institutional home.

Jenny (anxious but, nevertheless, more relaxed and somewhat more interested): Only with children?

Miss B.: No, it can also happen with young people. *(Pause.)* Are you afraid we could put you in a home?

Jenny (very meekly and softly): Can't you people here simply make decisions about me, like my parents?

Miss B.: Jenny, I'll tell you one thing: even if I could do that, I would not want to do it. Anyone who is pursuing a vocation and is expecting a baby is no longer a child. I have gotten the impression that you would be quite capable of helping decide what should happen now. First, you just need to become a little calmer again. *(Pause.)* Even if I have not been able to help a lot yet, perhaps you have, nonetheless, gained an understanding that the Youth Office is no police station. Unfortunately, I have no more time now to continue our conversation. There are, you see, a whole lot of "Jennys" who are in need and whom I would like to help. Would it be O.K. with you if you came to me again in a few days? You see, we have just met for the first time. I already think that I can help you, but for that I must know a little more about you—you'll understand that, won't you? *(Stands up, extends her hand to Jenny, who, somewhat self-consciously, grasps it with the same kind of curtsying movement.)* Would you like to come? On Friday?

Jenny (reflectively, seriously, and in a low voice): Oh, yes, I'll come for sure.

Why can we discover in this second dialogue—which obviously ends not in a catastrophe but full of promise—a basic attitude that establishes relationship?

1. The dialogue begins with an approach that is appropriate to the actual feelings of astonishment and resistance.

2. Right at the beginning, recognition is expressed for the achievement the client has made, even if this achievement consists only of coming into the office.

3. Very soon the fact that the partner is taken seriously is signaled by granting her the privilege of indicating whether certain meeting times are all right with her or not.

4. An attempt is made to pick up on possible experiences of success and happiness that Jenny has perhaps had in her work and to incorporate them into the dialogue.

5. Before the conversation really gets under way, factual information is given about what is supposed to happen in this dialogue, thereby clearing up some of the uncertainty and anxiety that occupies the client's mind.

6. The offer of help is made with the proviso that the client is free to make use of it or not.

7. The partner's emotional situation is clarified and made conscious in a way that apparently strikes her actual feelings, and therefore a renewed offer of help can also be made.

8. The doubt now expressed by the dialogue partner is received and confirmed, and in this way permission is also given for resistance and negative emotional attitudes to be articulated, to be spoken out and not shoved away or banned from the realm of dialogue.

9. The counselor does not answer the test question, which the client brings into play on her own, which throws open the question of guilt, and which is supposed to bring the social worker to an unambiguous decision for or against; instead, a fundamental rejection of a clarification of the guilt question is given, and thereby a new openness for further dialogue is signaled.

10. The social worker is in a position to admit her own helplessness and not set too demanding goals for the dialogue.

11. The client's hesitant offer of a somewhat emotional view of the Youth Office is not met with an unrealistic inflation of the social worker's own role and function; instead, information is given, and misconceptions are corrected.

12. The dialogue closes with an appeal to the client's own abilities, her own possibilities, and her own responsibility, thereby bringing into play the aspect of hope for the future. A relationship has been established on which one can now continue to build.

It should be clear that the essential difference between these two dialogues lies in the individual emotional attitudes of the respective social workers. A certain amount of control over one's own emotional reactions gives one the composure not to respond to the partner's emotional attitudes with the very same feelings and not to lose sight of the practical goal that has been set for the dialogue. As a methodological expansion of this basic attitude, we can also note the following about the two dialogues presented here: in the dialogue in which a relationship seems to have been successfully established, demands and appeals are employed very sparingly in the beginning, imperatives and admonishments are scarcely to be found, and placed at the client's disposal are a certain latitude and freedom to articulate her own feelings.

Now, however, the presupposition of the basic attitude that establishes relationship, as well as the methodological clarity with which such a dialogue is conducted, must be that we really understand the dialogue partner's communications.

GETTING THE MESSAGE

The psychoanalytic study of dialogue has repeatedly pointed out that words that are used in a dialogue, in addition to their linguistically conventional information content, have a secret meaning, a code character. What is said is at the same time an appeal to the person addressed to do something, to command, to lament, or to take under protection and defend.[3] The dialogue can become fruitful only if this meaning lying between the lines of the dialogue is perceived. I would like to illustrate this point with an example:[4]

> *The scene is a double room in a hospital. The patient is about thirty-five years old and has a well-kept appearance, hair in good shape, and elegant pajamas. He has a healthy self-consciousness and is open. After an introduction and a question about the patient's welfare, the following dialogue takes place.*
>
> *Patient:* I had an appendix operation; everything went well. I live in X and when abroad in M. Right now, I'm on vacation, so I took care of this thing right away.
>
> *Pastor:* Well, what is your job that takes you into S-land?
>
> *Patient:* I'm a representative of the large K firm and have a large territory in S-land. . . . You know, I've had all kinds of experience with the church; I'm sure you wouldn't understand.
>
> *Pastor:* Then, do you also have Protestant services there, in German?
>
> *Patient:* Yes, the V Church has made a chapel available to us. The Germans from the surrounding area come there. The pastor lives in Q. Naturally, he has a very large territory. So, one Sunday morning I come to church with my little daughter, a little early, and sit in a pew. Then here comes a German woman, an employee of the T Research Institute, and says to me, "Won't you make room for me?

That's my seat, you see." I stood up and left with my daughter and didn't participate in the service. I was so mad. You know, these employees of the T Institute have such huge salaries anyway; then they also get a discount of twenty percent in the big stores in the whole area. And then such a woman behaves like that in church. I haven't been back to the church again.

Pastor: Was that right?

Patient: I wrote about it to our pastor in Q. He gave me the right answer. You see, he wrote, "If someone in your firm had argued about your seat like that, would you have reacted in the same way?" But I also mean something else that I have experienced with the church. You won't believe it! We Germans in the whole surrounding area sent a common petition to Berlin, requesting that we have our own pastor. So they sent us a young pastor with his wife and three children. That was great for us. He visited all the Germans in the area. He also spent a whole evening with us; we visited leisurely over wine, and he stayed until 12:30. I said to my wife, "Now, that's a pastor who's just right for us." But it didn't work out. One day we were informed that he had been recalled.

Pastor: Why was that?

Patient: Worldly living! You can imagine how disappointed we were.

Pastor: Yes, but a pastor is only a human being. The congregation sometimes expects him to be a saint for whom there are no human temptations. But a pastor also lives by forgiveness. And where's the congregation that helps him then?

What can be perceived in this short dialogue? Obviously, the pastor has willingly followed the patient to the place where the patient wanted to lead him. That is, he let himself be forced into the position of a defender of church and pastor. With that the dialogue lost the chance to bring to expression this young man's central difficulty and need, which—in my view—underlies, as a code text, the young man's stories. We know from depth psychology that a person who is subject to the impulses and stirrings of his own unaccepted drives is inclined to transfer these impulses to others and fight them there. Now, this young man—who through the pastor's sudden appearance is caught in a somewhat defensive situation in which he moves decisively to counterattack—is obviously speaking about the subject and the problem that move him most deeply. He has, of course, no time to design a strategic plan to camouflage himself better, and therefore we may assume with some assurance that behind the reproach that he makes regarding the pastor of his congregation stand his own problems, which might have had a chance to be discovered if the pastor had only understood the code character of his patient's communications.

The actual difficulty of such short dialogues lies, of course, in summoning up the presence of mind to hear what is really being said and to react appropriately. This means not letting oneself be maneuvered into the role the dialogue partner has in mind for one but giving the dialogue a direction that will perhaps make it possible for what has previously been expressed only in a disguised and distorted way to be articulated openly. In this process, the following may be helpful.

As already indicated, it is precisely in short dialogues that it is very difficult to understand immediately the code character of utterances. Therefore we can largely restrict ourselves to focusing only on those words that seem to us to be loaded with emotion. Indeed, with a little practice and gift for observation, we will sense that in every dialogue there are certain parts and certain words that are brought forth in a different fashion from the rest of the dialogue text. Moser has recommended that such emotionally loaded words be called key words,[5] and he believes good prospects are offered by repeatedly throwing such key words into the conversation as long as possible, in order to stimulate the dialogue partner to new associations. Even if the reinjection of the key words into the dialogue situation does not stimulate new associations, the reaction of the dialogue partner to these words can still be extremely illuminating. That is, they are frequently retracted or flatly disavowed, or their use is even denied. We then have a confirmation of the fact that a definite emotional problem is actually hiding behind the key words, and we will now perhaps find a more appropriate means for dealing with it.

At this point, however, we face the question of what technical possibilities for conducting the dialogue stand at our disposal. As the most important means of directing dialogue we must name and discuss the question.

ASKING QUESTIONS

Out of the wealth of possible ways that questions can be employed in counseling—and out of the wealth of literature devoted to this topic[6]—I would like to discuss four basic types of questions that may be useful for our purposes:

(*a*) closed questions
(*b*) suggestive questions
(*c*) motivational questions
(*d*) open questions

(*a*) A closed question is one that can be adequately answered in a few words and therefore, as a rule, has no continuing function in the dialogue. We can distinguish different types of closed questions:

(i) The yes-no type represents a question that can be sufficiently answered with "yes" or "no," and then, as a rule, a new impulse or new activity from the counselor is required.

(ii) The identification type of closed question aims at the observable characteristics of people, places, objects, and events, identified in terms of time, number, and so forth. Such identification questions begin with interrogative words like "who," "where," "when," "how many," and "which."

(iii) By the selection type of closed question we mean the fixed-alternative question that leaves the respondent the choice between two possibilities—for example, "Do you have pain or just discomfort?"

(iv) The subjective type of closed question tries to move the counselee to very definite expressions of convictions or feelings and thus to direct the identification inward, so to speak.

(*b*) Suggestive questions bring to expression in some way or other the fact that the expectations of the questioner lie in a particular direction. The respondent is thus forced into a decision as to whether he wants to fulfill these expectations or put up a defense against them. Here too we can distinguish four different types:

(i) The passive type of suggestive question only introduces the object of the inquiry—for example, "Do you have pain?"

(ii) The active type of suggestive question goes yet a step further and introduces even more strongly the expected answer: "You have pain, don't you?"

(iii) With the subjective type of suggestive question, which places subjective perception or feeling in the center, the suggestive effect can be regulated, for example, in the following way. One can ask, "Did you see an umbrella?" or "Did you see *the* umbrella?" or "Didn't you see an umbrella?" or "Didn't you see *the* umbrella?"

(iv) A further intensification of the suggestive effect can be achieved by forming the suggestive question in an objective way, that is, no longer according to subjective perceptions or feelings but according to objective facts, as in the following levels of intensity, for example: "Was there an umbrella there?" "Was there not an umbrella there?" "Was the umbrella black or gray?" "Was the umbrella black?"

(*c*) Motivational questions constitute the third general category. They are exclusively *why* questions, and their special problem consists in the fact that they especially tempt one only to give the conscious reasons for an action but not to offer elucidation about the real inner motives. They lure the counselee into rationalization and almost always evoke a desire for justification. A large proportion of *why* questions cannot be answered by the dialogue partner at all, and therefore such questions lead, with extraordinary frequency, to breaks in the dialogue.

(*d*) The open question—which only stakes out the field of inquiry, as it were—is a question that requires more than a few words to be answered intentionally and which basically leaves everything open—for example, "Please, can you tell me what brings you here?"

Now, with the exception of the opening question of a dialogue, all the questions that are asked in the course of the conversation have a reference to what has gone before. This reference can be established in manifold ways as required by the dialogue situation. Thus we must ask ourselves in what ways questions can be related to their points of reference. I mention the following possibilities:

1. The echo is an exact repetition of the words of the dialogue partner, with only a question mark added. This is the process that will generally be used in picking up on key words.

2. Extension involves a request to expand, extend, or go into more detail on information already given.

3. In indirect clarification a request is made for a piece of information that was already implicitly included in an earlier part of the dialogue but not yet specifically put into words.

4. In direct clarification it is a matter of a direct request for information about something that has previously remained vague and ambiguous but is part of a topic clearly addressed.

5. With a summarizing question, a particular section of the dialogue can be marked off. It can be tied to an implicit or explicit request for confirmation.

6. Confrontation involves a question that calls direct attention to a contradiction in the utterances of the dialogue partner.

7. Finally, there can also be the repetition of a question that has already been posed and which seems to us not sufficiently answered.

This completes the description of the arsenal, so to speak, that we have available in the technique of questioning in a dialogue. Later we will go more into the details of the application of these means; here we have only marked out with broad strokes how they may come into play.

For our purposes, the most inappropriate type must be the closed question, since it leads too easily to the wrong procedure: interrogation. It breaks up the dialogue into tiny dialogue particles and constantly interrupts its flow. Likewise, we must be clear about the problems of the suggestive question. It should be employed only when we can relate it to a clear intention. That intention will consist mainly in the emotional unburdening of our dialogue partner. If we ask our partner, "You have certainly been through all kinds of things in your life, haven't you?" we are posing, of course, a suggestive question. It then seems possible and appropriate if it leads to the partner's being able to confess emotional stirrings to himself and perhaps bring them to expression. For practical purposes, the motivational question is excluded as a possibility in the pastoral dialogue. One should seek to avoid it in all cases.

Thus there remains, as the primary instrument in the pastoral dialogue, the open question, which in certain cases may have the character of giving concrete information, which gives our partner the opportunity to express emotional reactions, and which, by being related and directed to particular aspects of what has already been said, can afford the partner a little insight into his own problems. No one should venture into counseling who has not made an attempt, at least a few times, to write down a word-for-word transcription, to underline all the interrogatives he has used, and to examine their legitimacy.

We have yet to point to one final aspect of the question technique, namely, the question of truthfulness. The surveys that have dealt so intensively with sexual activities—for example, those of Kinsey—have often been subjected to the criticism that a question technique was used that can no longer be considered proper, because it presupposes something that does not necessarily correspond with the truth. As an example thereof, one could recall that classic scene from *Hamlet* in which the question is whether one can catch the "carp of truth" with the "bait of falsehood."[7] In the case of the Kinsey questionnaires, the issue was that a particular presupposition was made that had not yet been communicated by the respondent. Thus one was not asked, "Do you masturbate?" but rather, "How long have you been masturbating?" In certain cases even in a pastoral dialogue it can sometimes facilitate matters if we presuppose, as obviously accepted by us, something that our partner apparently cannot express at all or only with difficulty, because he has feelings of guilt. Nonetheless, this cannot go so far that we abandon truthfulness to ourselves and perhaps outflank and push aside unrecognized guilt feelings that prevent the expression of certain things. In any case, it is better to find out why someone can discuss certain themes only with difficulty than to devise a refined technique that can clear away or circumvent this barrier without our learning why it was actually erected.

GIVING ANSWERS

Our task in this section is to discover the significance for the dialogue itself of the answers we give in counseling. When in the following we propose a value scale for the answers of the counselor, this valuation is made not on the basis of content categories but from the standpoint of how these answers affect the dialogue that follows, that is, how they activate a sort of psychic feedback mechanism. The counselor must bear in mind that each of his answers represents a verbal conditioning of the subsequent dialogue. According to experimental investigations, we can establish the following scale of the conditioning effect of our own utterances:[8]

1. The injection of our own experiences shows itself to have the greatest effect on the dialogue and on its continuation. Wherever the counselor reacts to his counselee's presentation of a problem with his own experience, he must reckon with the fact that the partner will receive this personal experience as a kind of norm that he must either orient himself toward or must absolutely reject and return by means of a more negative transference. From the standpoint of the continued leadership of the dialogue and the provocation of further communications from the partner, the injection of personal experiences must, therefore, be regarded as an unsuitable means of doing counseling. Hence, it appears permissible only in cases where the end of the dialogue is in sight and where we also do not intend to continue with a series of further sessions.

2. The situation is similar with regard to the use of foreign examples. As far as the dialogue is concerned, even citing the experience of others proves to be an urging to orient oneself positively or negatively toward this experience and thus, as a rule, blocks the communication of additional experiences of one's own.

3. Our own value judgments and positions also cannot emerge in the dialogue situation until the partner's communications have reached a certain closure, when further communications are not

expected and also should no longer be evoked. At this point the dialogue enters a new phase that might involve a discussion of the counselor's views regarding previously expressed experiences and information.

4. The answering of questions posed to the counselor must be handled in a similar fashion. As long as the presumption persists that such questions come from the anxiety and insecurity of the partner and represent no genuine need for information, a valid and informative response to such questions cannot be approved. In such a case, it seems more effective and sensible either to give the question back to the questioner—which, naturally, will result in a certain amount of frustration (and one must wonder whether the questioner can handle such frustration at this moment)—or to consider together what function this question now has for the whole dialogue in general, why it was asked, and what perhaps still not fully conscious motives lie behind it. Not until these issues are clarified to some extent, of course, can the dialogue move to giving answers that will raise the possibility of closing off one area of consideration and pushing on to further topics.[9]

In contrast to these four possibilities are four more that can evoke and stimulate a continuation of the dialogue:

1. The first is summarization. If the counselor has the feeling that a particular theme or a particular set of problems has been exhausted and that further information is not to be expected here, it has proved to be extremely helpful if he attempts a summary of the dialogue up to that point, which may possibly be accompanied by a request to the partner to confirm or validate the counselor's understanding of the present situation in the dialogue. But one must bear in mind that such a summary, of necessity, operates selectively, that it chooses and emphasizes certain aspects of previously presented material, and thus in a decisive way determines the future course of the dialogue.

2. Some steering of the dialogue's course is especially recommended when the partner is not practiced in the art of verbal expression, when his thoughts and associations so overwhelm

him that there is almost a flood of ideas and there is a danger that the dialogue will overflow its banks, so to speak, and dissolve into a formless pool. It can be helpful here to give special emphasis to themes that the counselor underlines and lifts out with specific brief remarks.

3. This accentuation and affirmation of certain themes and objects need not be accomplished through the verbal remarks of the counselor. Even affirmation by means of agreeing sounds such as "Hm!" or something similar—as empirical research has shown[10]—can stimulate and influence the partner more or less consciously, so that these themes will appear more often in the later course of the dialogue. Under experimental conditions researchers affirmed the use of plural forms in dialogue with an agreeing "Hm!" and were able to demonstrate statistically that thereafter the use of plural forms in the dialogue increased considerably as compared to a dialogue situation in which this emphatic affirmation was not given.

4. Finally, the counselor must understand that there are also nonverbal answers on his part—a nod of the head or a tense facial expression or an expression of indifferent absentmindedness. All of these things are quite often anxiously followed by the counselee and also have an unconscious effect to the extent that topics and words affirmed and emphasized through nonverbal communication appear more often than other, unstressed ones in the later course of the dialogue.

The conscious steering of one's own answers in dialogue serves the single purpose of letting the steering of the dialogue's course—by the one whose task is to lead the dialogue—occur as consciously as possible. It is an illusion to assume that such a steering through the answers of the counselor can be completely eliminated. Whoever believes this is a long way from a realistic estimation of the dialogue situation and will therefore, without noticing it, have an effect of guidance and possibly of authoritarian determination on his dialogue partner. The more we make ourselves conscious of our own utterances and the clearer we are about the use of our own answers, the more nondirectively the dialogue will proceed; that is, the danger will be somewhat diminished that what the dialogue leader questions his counselee about, and stimulates him to talk about, will be only what he himself wants to hear and what meets his expectations.

DEALING WITH METHODOLOGICAL PLURALISM

The practical problems that have been raised thus far bring us to a fundamental question. From what areas of research can the pastor adopt systematic instructions for counseling without being untrue to his fundamental theological principles, according to which he should facilitate for his dialogue partner, and exercise together with him, the greatest possible amount of freedom? The problem is made especially difficult by the fact that in recent years scientific research into the methodology of counseling has expanded at an almost explosive rate. Thus there can be no more talk of pastoral care's having only one dialogue partner, namely, psychology, but instead one must distinguish very clearly between various methods of counseling, which rest in turn on various, and in part considerably divergent, theoretical models. Faced with such a confusing pluralism of methodology, the pastor has only one course of action. With the help of theological criteria and on the basis of his specific dialogue goals, he must make a decision: To which of the available methods would he like to entrust the proceedings? Which method or combination of methods seems to him reasonable and feasible? We would, therefore, like to close this chapter with a short overview of the three most important methodological approaches and their theological evaluation.

Behavior-therapy-oriented counseling. The first to speak of behavior therapy were Arnold A. Lazarus and Hans Jürgen Eysenck, independently of each other in 1958 and 1959.[11] Thus we have here a relatively young form of therapy that, nevertheless, seeks to make use of one of the oldest practices of humanity, namely, the attempt "to influence and shape the behavior of at least its younger and weaker members through reward, punishment, withholding attention, or by having old contents appear in new contexts."[12] What is new in this method is that, through the accumulation of a large body of research, learning processes have been made interpretable as an interplay between the individual and his environment which is subject to certain regularities. Close at hand lay the conjecture that it must be possible "through a systematic influencing of this interplay so to modify behavior that, given the individual possibilities of a person, the things that are more in accord with reality and more efficient will be strengthened, while those that are disturbing and more inefficient will be weakened."[13] This conjecture was confirmed through a wealth of experiments that—building on Pavlov's famous "conditioned reflexes"—were carried out at first with animals but also increasingly with human beings. There can be no doubt at all that clearly definable methods such as classical conditioning, desensitization, aversion therapy, operant conditioning, reinforcement techniques, punishment, extinction, stimulus control, and model learning—to name only the most important[14]—can have an effective and probably even long-term influence on human behavior. Desirable behavior can thus be induced through "reinforcements" that can be applied as subtle forms of reward, and undesirable behavior can gradually be stemmed through punishment.

To be sure, it has been demonstrated that all methods of punishment unleash anxiety and aggression[15] and only lead to a situation-dependent suppression of behavior; only the "systematic and continuing withdrawal of all concern by withholding attention," which "can cause many disturbing modes of behavior to disappear,"[16] has proved successful as a long-term form of therapy. Clearly, however, the reward is and remains the most important behavior therapy measure, and in this connection it has been learned that the best example of a "secondary reinforcement" is money. Thus many behavior-therapy institutions work with their own monetary system, for which there must be as large as possible a number of exchange opportunities interesting to the patient. Experience has shown, however, that every kind of personal attention, be it ever so subtle, comes into play as social reinforcement and reward. Thus in this respect behavior therapy undertakes a transfer of responsibility to the patient in order to let him experience for himself the consequences of his actions, which wait for him as reward and punishment.[17]

Naturally, with this program, behavior therapy very quickly found itself exposed to a crossfire of criticism. Above all, it has been subjected to the reproach of manipulation because of its effort to set into operation, assured by the superior force of effective methodology, its system of behavioral influence, even against the will of the patient, if necessary. Under the pressure of this criticism, behavior therapy found it necessary to turn increased attention to the question of achieving therapeutic goal settings and the related evaluations. Since efforts are made, as far as possible, to determine together with the patient exactly "what in his behavior is to be changed in what way"[18] "so that the client can make a decision on the basis of genuine information, . . . ethical concerns because of manipulative tendencies are without foundation."[19]

A further critical objection, that behavior therapy treats manifest behavior disorders but not their hidden cause, is largely dismissed with the concise remark that the patient comes, indeed, only for the sake of eliminating his prominent symptoms, and thus under no circumstances could a more thorough treatment be forced upon him. The question of whether only a shifting of symptoms and no lasting healing is realized will not be answerable until sufficient time has passed to allow the long-term results of therapy to be empirically verified.

For our purposes, however, the following question is of interest. As far as I know, there are as yet no programmatic and planned attempts to adopt the methods of behavior therapy in the practice of pastoral care, although in the near future they will certainly have to be reckoned with. A thorough reflection on the methodological means and aims of behavior therapy, however, can serve the pastor in another way: it can make him conscious of how often he avails himself of behavior-therapy methods without being conscious of it or making himself methodologically accountable for it. Whenever a subject that comes up in the dialogue seems to be especially important to the pastor and he shows increased attention, increased interest, and increased concern, he, often without suspecting it, is making use of social reinforcement, which causes his client, often equally unconsciously, to dwell on this theme or to return to it. Whenever in a dialogue particular behavior of the client is met with a lessening of the intensity of concern, something like "aversion therapy" occurs, which leads to the suppression of this behavior or a turning of attention away from this topic. It seems to me that an uncovering of the laws that govern emotional learning processes provides the key to understanding psychic reversals as they play a role in conversion experiences and lately can also be observed in religious movements such as the "Jesus people."

Interpreted theologically, this could mean that behavior therapy and religious orthodoxy have a point of contact in an anthropological pessimism that leads to a complete absolutization of the *extra nos*. The solution to the problem is expected either from a preformulated treatment goal or from a preformulated religious answer, toward which one is conditioned, consciously or unconsciously, with the help of social reinforcement. The personal contribution of the counselee within the therapeutic or pastoral process itself must thereby sink to a minimum; freedom in the sense of an expansion of consciousness will be impossible to achieve.

Client-centered therapy. It is therefore all too understandable that, almost as the complete antitype of behavior therapy, a form of therapy was developed that has sought, since the appearance of behavior therapy, to define itself ever more strongly as the opposite pole. Begun by the American psychologist Carl Rogers[20] and at first called the "nondirective" method, later "client-centered therapy," and today often shortened to "dialogue therapy," it has already to a large extent become the basic model for pastoral procedure, especially in the United States. In contrast to behavior therapy, dialogue therapy in no way starts out with a treatment goal already formulated regarding content; its goal is, if need be, "to make possible for the client a clarification of his own feelings, wishes, and value concepts and to put him thereby in a position to interact more effectively with his environment in accordance with his goals."[21]

In its theoretical concept this form of therapy concentrates its interest notably on the problem of anxiety and especially on its social components. Regarded as the core problem of the client's difficulties are fears that bring a person to the point of not being able to cope in many everyday situations, as well as the fear of any change in his inward or outward circumstances, "which prevents the client from striking out alone on new paths toward overcoming problems."[22] The first law of dialogue therapy, therefore, is to establish an atmosphere of anxiety-free communication in which the client is neither "shocked" through unexpected interpretations or explanations, nor "attacked" with an indication that he may be wrong in his way of looking at things. Top priority is given to a clarification of present and immediate feelings; every reference to the past is expressly rejected. Basically, the client himself determines the content of the therapeutic dialogue and is supposed to reach the point where he himself "in small steps" actively clears the path toward a solution to his difficulties. Thus, as the goal of therapy, there emerges not a certain desired behavior but simply greater freedom from fear, greater inner freedom, a strengthened acceptance of oneself and one's weaknesses, greater emotional security, self-reliance, independence, flexibility, and initiative.

These improved possibilities for living, nevertheless, are not brought to the client from the outside but are the result of a kind of "self-exploration" by the client through which he, with the help of the therapist, becomes better acquainted with his own feelings and also with his own inner possibilities, which have perhaps previously lain fallow. In order to reach this common goal, the therapist has imposed upon him a certain catalogue of modes of behavior that he must make his own with the help of critical evaluation through individual or group supervision. With his positive estimation of worth and emotional warmth toward the client, through his genuine and open behavior, his active participation and his relaxed and anxiety-free demeanor that encourages new ways of looking at things, the therapist is supposed to facilitate a verbalization of the client's experiences and at the same time serve as model of relaxed, problem-solving behavior. Dialogue therapy has made especially popular the basic function of "mirroring," which, with the aid of an easily learned technique, confronts the client repeatedly with his currently present feelings and gives them back to him for further comments.

We must certainly welcome the idea of a pastor's learning, through a certain amount of training like that in dialogue therapy, to control his modes of behavior that are unconsciously suggestive and thereby conditioning in the sense of behavior therapy. Nevertheless, the problems with which the client-centered method confronts us are very great. With the strong concentration on the current emotional situation and on currently persisting anxieties, as well as the total rejection of a biographical arrangement and any interpretation of the origins of improper modes of behavior, the client is left almost exclusively with the here and now of his present situation. This brings with it the danger that what is actually intended—namely, the discovery of new possibilities for resolving a conflict situation—cannot be achieved; but, instead, the client unconsciously and unintentionally reaches back into the past for the model of behavior with which he most strongly identifies. An attentive study of dialogue analyses and transcripts, such as those provided for pastoral areas by Heije Faber and Ebel van der Schoot,[23] shows that the solution of the conflict situation described therein almost always works in the same way as the educational forces of the past and thus means no real freedom and no really new experience.

Hence, one could say that client-centered therapy allows the suspicion of an anthropological optimism that simply leaves the client dependent on himself and his current possibilities. The crippling and enslaving power of past experiences could thus be overlooked and the struggle for freedom not deeply enough joined. The knowledge could be suppressed that only by means of a meaning-imparting interpretation is freedom from the compulsion to repeat possible, and one could underestimate the significance of the *extra nos* of a counselor who not only functions as a mirror but is also present as an actual partner.

Counseling oriented toward depth psychology. We have already given expression more than once to the fact that we consider indispensable the cognizance and incorporation of psychoanalytical ways of thinking in the counseling to be practiced in pastoral care. In this connection, with regard to the counseling of behavior therapy and client-centered therapy, only the following points will be mentioned. If we saw on the one hand an anthropological pessimism that led to an absolutization of the *extra nos* as the authority that is significant and important for the client, so must we, on the other hand, ascertain an anthropological optimism that leads to the elimination of those elements that in the Christian tradition are expressed with the term *extra nos.* Thus the problem is to find that theoretical concept which represents something like an anthropological realism that leads to a situation where the element of help coming from the outside does not succeed at the cost of one's own psychic resources and avenues of help. These requirements seem to me to be met by several elements in the theory of depth psychology, which in this connection, therefore, are once again summarized.

1. Klaus Winkler has recently pointed out that basic to a depth-psychological viewpoint—no matter to which school it might be ascribed—is a model of personality that is based on the idea that some individual human drives and strivings are not accepted by the conscious mind and as a result of this suppression are represented consciously only through conflicts and symptoms. The appropriate therapy would then aim at "bringing about a new and different interaction with the parts of the personality that are inhibited or repressed into the unconscious."[24] Arising against this, however, is the resistance of the client, with the same intensity that once led to the rejection of the repressed parts of the personality. It seems to me that with the mention of the resistance that arises against any implementation of a helping relationship—whether it is of the therapeutic or the pastoral type—we have brought into the discussion an anthropological realism that neither deprives the client of his own fundamental ability to deal with what is important to him nor maintains that with the return to the client himself and to his own feelings,

the essential has already happened. With the assertion that human resistance arises against any expansion of consciousness and thus also against any change of consciousness, it seems to me that depth psychology comes very close to certain fundamental biblical anthropological insights. Corresponding to this, in my opinion, is the recognition that pastoral counseling must also reckon with such resistance, that it must include resistance in its methodological deliberations and have at its disposal suitable equipment for the appropriate consideration and treatment of resistance.

2. The suitable instrument of this treatment of resistance in depth psychology in general is reflective interaction with transference. We have, therefore, pointed out the attendant circumstances in such detail, in order to make clear that in every case they also play a role in the pastoral relationship. Now, they also allow a religious interpretation. As we tried to show with the example of the Freudian interpretation of the healing of the paralytic,[25] the invitation to unlimited transference is not a human, and thus not a pastoral, possibility. It is rather a question of disillusioning, in the truest sense, the transference expectations and hopes of the client[26] and of transforming them into a relationship based on reality instead of the compulsion to repeat.

3. According to the theory of depth psychology, this function is taken over largely by interpretation. It is more than the "self-exploration" conceived in dialogue therapy.[27] It tries rather to take what impedes the dialogue situation as meaningless resistance and, by drawing in transference and countertransference phenomena, make it understandable as a meaningful compulsion to repeat, and also bring it into a context of meaning beyond the individual with the help of models that have been gathered by the history of human experience and preserved in the great documents of religious experience. What a person has experienced with his father, and what he also experiences allusively through transference in his relationship with the pastor, is now no longer meaningless personal fate but meaningful "oedipal" experience. What he experienced as refusal through his mother is no longer her individual inability but the common body of

experience of all the "orally frustrated" who had to leave the fleshpots of Egypt for the privations and uncertain wandering of the wilderness. In my view, it appears to be this ordering into a meaningful whole that transforms unsayable and as yet unheard things into meaningful experience with a fellow human being; it enables the client gradually to give up the implementation of his infantile wishes, to mollify his resistance, to break away from the compulsion to repeat with eternal sameness; and it allows the hope slowly to grow in him that even he can have new experiences and can change his world so that possibilities of happiness are available to him.

5. Critical Points in Counseling

THESIS: A responsible counselor must keep in mind that every counseling session evokes anxiety. One must have at one's disposal adequate conceptual models that can offer help in observing, interpreting, and perhaps influencing the development of anxiety. Also, the possible effects of the dialogue on the social environment must be considered. The dangers of acting out feelings, breaking off the dialogue, and developing potential dependencies must be seen in relation to their causes and appropriately answered.

Previously we pleaded for a stronger awareness in dialogue and have, up to this point, put the emphasis on observing and making conscious one's own reactions; and we have focused attention on the conscious application of a question technique and the effect of one's own possible answers. Now we must also extend this attention to the dialogue partner and turn to the following questions: What does the dialogue mean for him? What inner processes have perhaps been set in motion within him? In this regard it must be noted that the subjective reaction to the dialogue situation is always twofold. On the one hand, every new and unknown situation more or less consciously evokes anxiety. On the other hand, a dialogue can call forth extraordinary feelings of satisfaction. We will be able to understand these emotional reactions of the client, which remain mostly unconscious and unspoken, only if we can paint ourselves a general picture of what is going on inside him. Especially suited for this purpose is the conceptual model of the psyche that psychoanalysis has drawn.

A little-regarded additional consideration is the fact that every dialogue, especially when it stretches over a longer period of time, has an effect on the social environment of the counselee. One must keep clearly in mind that the possibility is very great that a confidential relationship outside the family situation could have a reciprocal effect back into that situation. It is the unanimous experience of all developmental and marriage counseling that having such a dialogue leads at first not to any relief in the social situation but rather to its becoming more acute. Since with the pastor or counselor the partner feels himself accepted and understood, it may be easier for his aggressive impulses to be acted out in the social environment, and we often find that the parents or spouse will turn to the pastor or counselor full of horror because the anticipated improvement has not come about at all, but rather an intensification of the problem.

Very often the dialogue also leads to particular actions of the dialogue partner that occur either outside or inside the dialogue situation and that are directly related to certain causes in the counseling situation. This acting-out of the dialogue partner has until now received far too little attention. Quite frequently it offers the key to understanding very difficult dialogue situations. In any case, it is in the background in the breaking-off of dialogue and in the behavior of the "clinging vine," the person who cannot accept the dialogue situation as a partnership of limited duration but wants to extend the relationship ad infinitum. We would like to bring all these points once again to conscious observation and consideration as critical situations within counseling.

THE PROBLEM OF ANXIETY IN DIALOGUE

In its early years psychoanalysis developed a concept of anxiety that, in a manner similar to that of Søren Kierkegaard, connected anxiety with the instinctive drives within the human psyche.[1] The observation that Freud made with his patients, that anxiety can appear in the place of libidinous instinct, led to the hasty presumption that libido is transformed into anxiety; but later on, this theory of anxiety had to be altered and reversed. Following

Kierkegaard's distinction, anxiety and fear were differentiated, and the thesis was proposed that fear is a reaction to an external, perceivable source of danger, whereas anxiety represents a danger signal in response to an inner threat. This inner threat must be regarded as that situation in which the ego of the conscious personality either is flooded by the instinctive realm of the id or is so constricted by the similarly unconscious realm of the superego that it is overcome by the affect of anxiety.

Now, this conceptual model of the human psyche will also prove helpful if we want to convey what sort of anxiety it is that almost always plays a role in dialogue. From a first, superficial glance, one could get the impression that it is anxiety over the strangeness and newness of the situation or the concern at being brought into an unpleasant situation by an unknown new dialogue partner. After a closer look and more profound experience of the dialogue situation, however, we must assume that the anxiety that manifests itself in the dialogue is related to instinctive drives within the human psyche. Even in the dialogue situation we can observe hints of instinctive processes. We distinguish two fundamental groupings: (1) those instinctive impulses that come from the id and lead to an attempt in some way to take possession of the dialogue partner, and (2) the instinctive impulses that come from the superego and show an identification tendency, the goal of which is to be like the partner in the dialogue.

In regard to the first grouping—that is, takeover tendencies, which may make themselves known in very subtle ways—we must again distinguish two different possibilities: either a domination of the aggressive basic structure or a domination of the libidinous basic structure. If the dialogue partner attempts to carry out his takeover tendency, then he will see in the aggressive basic structure of his partner an ally in aggression that he has against other possible partners or related persons on the outside. The counselee seeks aggressively to take possession of the counselor or pastor and tries, through all kinds of actions and demeanor, to provoke a certain behavior from the counselor, to force him into a certain role, to cause him to take certain measures. In the domination of the structure of libidinous drives, the counselee tries to put himself into an infantile dependency relationship and in this way take possession of the counselor libidinously by trying intensively to appeal to his willingness to help, his good-heartedness, his pity. In this category, we have already become acquainted with the masochistic triumph. The dynamic tendency of such a dialogue is to entangle the counselor or pastor in instinctual impulses. The result is a general swelling of the realm of instinct, which is powerfully stimulated. This means, however, a weakening of the ego, and the outcome of this tendency in any case is increased anxiety.

We have already pointed to the fact that the anxiety of the counselee can also stimulate the anxiety of the counselor, so that at this point he is repeatedly in danger of making certain errors in conducting the dialogue. We can perhaps summarize these in the following way: such mistaken behavior can consist in giving the counselee justification in his struggle against some related person, or on the counselor's part, in reacting aggressively to the aggressive tendencies of the partner, or in seeking to take possession of the counselee, taking him under wing, actively reaching into his life and trying to shape him, or in increasing attention according to the demands of the counselee. Thus the dynamic of such a relationship will lead to a steady growth in demands until they increase at an avalanchelike rate. We must make an effort to recognize such anxiety-developing tendencies early on, so that we can influence and guide them. This will occur by not offering one's own convictions and judgments, by not letting oneself be provoked to emotional reactions, by not actively giving advice, and by not permitting the intensity of concern to undergo any variations, but instead by making known that one is ready to accept the counselee even in his anxiety, by seeking to provide for an even temperature in the emotional climate, by expressing a steady interest in everything that the counselee presents and by making available a clearly defined area of concern. With that, we ask the counselee to refuse the instinctual level, but we offer him another experience of satisfaction that lies on the level of the ego. We offer him the prospect, namely, that we can come to a better understanding of the counselee himself, of any related persons, and of the situation. Thereby something that appeared at the very least threatening becomes comprehensible, and so the effect is to relax the anxiety.

The identification tendency conceals similar dangers and is also possible with aggressive and libidinous dominance. It leads in aggressive dominance to that recognized phenomenon which Anna Freud has called identification with the aggressor;[2] that is, the dialogue partner perceives the counselor or pastor in every case as an aggressive element but tries to escape him by identifying with him. With libidinous dominance the result is a passive submission that is repeatedly expressed, for example, in the following way of speaking: "Please, just tell me what I've done wrong! Tell me what I should do!" The tendency of such a dialogue is to turn the counselor or pastor into the superego of the counselee. In this way a new thrust toward repression would be introduced, a new constriction of the ego would occur, and new anxieties would be released. This tendency can be reinforced and intensified by the wrong behavior in the dialogue situation. It must be seen as incorrect behavior when the pastor or counselor tries to comply with the tendencies of his partner and attempts to be very nice to him, when he lets himself be moved to moral judgments or tries to shape the counselee and manipulate him in certain directions. Also, stepping too hastily into the specifically pastoral role, by which one makes oneself the superego of the other, will have disastrous consequences at this point. For the inner dynamic of this dialogue situation consists in a vicious circle, where anxieties originate from guilt feelings and guilt feelings from anxieties. Instead of this, the pastor or counselor must always be himself and never let himself be maneuvered into a role that is foreign to him; that is, he must not let himself be bound to a judgment but also not let himself be led into untruthfulness. He takes the wishes that are made to him and for the time being returns them as questions to the one concerned, and he has clearly in mind that the pastoral element consists initially in the embodiment of an acceptance of the person who comes to him. Thus once again a refusal is demanded in that we reject the role of the superego, but we hold forth the prospect of offering our help to master the realm of freedom. In a competent partnership over a period of time we can make an effort to take the life of another to some extent into our care and help to dismantle illusionary feelings of guilt. Anxiety and guilt are constant companions in dialogue situations in which there is a helping relationship. We can transform this care into a mutual human experience and thereby work to alleviate anxiety.[3]

EFFECTS ON THE SOCIAL ENVIRONMENT

Every dialogue situation, especially when it is a matter of a series of sessions held over a long period of time, has a feedback effect on the social environment in which the counselee lives. Many such social environments are very carefully balanced systems of relationships that immediately fall into disorder when an outside person is drawn into this sphere.[4] As a rule the pastoral or counseling relationship at first means a strengthening of the one who undertakes it. Therefore, in his social connections he also feels somewhat stronger and able to be more aggressive, to become more active, to become more critical. Hence, changes occur in these areas of social relationships as an indirect consequence of the dialogue situation. Especially if the pastor makes contact with other persons in the social sphere, he runs the risk of becoming involved in its dynamic interaction of forces. He gets played off against others. Frequently such situations then become so muddled that one can scarcely extricate oneself.

We must therefore make clear methodologically what possibilities are at our disposal here:

1. The easiest and clearest possibility, when we are faced with a family conflict, is to establish contact with only one person from this arena of conflict and steadfastly refuse to make other contacts. If the wish comes up that other persons in the conflict be drawn into the counseling, then it is absolutely necessary to have someone else brought in to do the counseling. We can then to some extent rely on the fact that the information

we receive comes from one person; we also feel ourselves to be the partner of this one person and will try to help him further in dialogue and thereby achieve an indirect effect back into the social environment.

2. The second possibility would be joint counseling. This involves two people coming for counseling at the same time or one after the other. In this dialogue situation, one must from the very beginning give consideration to the fact that it represents a triangular situation. Only in a three-way dialogue can it actually be brought to a satisfactory conclusion.

3. Joint counseling by two counselors is to be recommended when there is an extremely serious conflict situation—marriage conflict or parent-child conflict—and when this conflict situation is marked by the forceful subjugation and domination of one of the two partners. In these situations it proves helpful in such four-way dialogues for each of the dialogue partners to have his own counselor, to whom, as a rule, he can address himself especially. Such four-way situations can be separated into two-way dialogues and, as needed, be brought together again as four-way discussions.

4. Finally, the pinnacle of pastoral counseling work is group counseling of the whole social field. It is carried on in the United States but requires from the counselor a great deal of supervision and self-control. Thus, given the present educational conditions in pastoral counseling that we have in Germany, it is excluded as a practical possibility but, of course, represents an ideal form of counseling.

Let us ask ourselves what happens when the series of dialogues has progressed as we would like, when the ego has been strengthened, when understanding has been expanded, when a certain maturation has indeed been accomplished. The feedback effect on the social environment will then consist in a certain distance vis-à-vis this environment, but especially in an insight into what really happens there, and finally, in a change of our own attitude and the possibility of influencing the attitudes of others. In any case, our goal in regard to the social field will be an emotional unburdening and an understanding of action and reaction in the dynamic interaction of forces and social needs.

EFFECTS ON THE COUNSELING SITUATION

Now that we have made clear the effects of the dialogue on the social environment and have recognized that the dialogue can lead to actions outside the counseling situation, we would like to clarify the counselee's actions in a more limited sense, namely, changes in the counseling situation that come about through the emotional swings in the psyche of our dialogue partner. We have seen that as a rule they have something to do with our partner's anxiety, which, moreover, is a signal that affective expressions of emotion threaten to invade the counseling situation. They may be of either the aggressive or the libidinous type. It will be very important to assess as soon as possible our partner's emotional situation and to be able to respond to it with help, if needed. Therefore we shall distinguish three large groupings that will help us recognize the acting-out of our dialogue partner in counseling:[5]

(*a*) changes in the modulation of communication
(*b*) changes in the intensity of communication
(*c*) changes in the content of communication

(*a*) By changes in the modulation of communication we mean all those small, scarcely perceivable signs that something is happening to the feelings of the other person. They can be expressed even in frequent coughing or clearing of the throat, which is always a sign that the one concerned is experiencing a certain amount of emotional tension. They are expressed in voice changes: I recently had to conduct a dialogue—which, to be sure, came very close to being an examination situation—in which the person was apparently moved by anxiety and insecurity to the point where the voice migrated higher and higher into the head and lost all resonance in the diaphragm and abdomen. Very hasty and excited speaking as well as sudden lengthenings in one's speech point to the fact that strong feelings have come into play and are influencing the partner's willingness to communicate.

(*b*) Changes in the intensity of communication can become noticeable when my partner's train of thought suddenly comes to a stop, when he expresses surprising signs of fatigue or begins to yawn, and when, finally, the dialogue runs down into silence. Moser has pointed out that a pause is often the result of a suppression of painful ideas.[6] It occurs in order to avoid the breaking-through of emotion stimulated by the dialogue. In it lies a challenge to the dialogue leader to take over the active leadership of the dialogue. My partner is changing from the spontaneous assertion of his emotional position to its passive defense. He is attempting a shift in roles. When we make clear to ourselves and have no questions about the fact that a pause could be an expression of anxiety that the strength of affect is reaching the point where it could become explicit, or on the other hand, that talking about a feeling could disturb one's secret enjoyment of this mood, then it is clear that verbalization can serve the unloading or the restriction of emotions. Therefore it is a component of affect control.

Likewise, a pause and the endurance of a pause, naturally, can increase enormously the tension in the dialogue. When one waits out a pause, this means taking in the bargain an enormously high level of tension. Harald Schultz-Hencke names five reasons for silence:[7] first, in the background is a personal secret that one does not intend to give up; second, one wants to protect the secret of another person; third, criticism of the partner; fourth, criticism of the procedure and fear of a possible, imagined result; fifth, pronounced positive feelings for the dialogue partner. With this background it becomes clear that the question of how long one can endure a pause without comment is an extraordinarily important question. Empirical research has shown that a pause of about three to ten seconds does not substantially harm the intensity of the communication that begins after the pause, but that after a pause that lasts more than ten seconds, the dialogue partner is inclined to give shorter answers.[8] The longer the silence continues, the less is the chance that it will be ended by the dialogue partner. The likelihood that the dialogue leader himself will become anxious and for that reason endeavor to get the dialogue moving again as soon as possible very often causes a change of subject and thus a gap in the dialogue.

A propitious ending to a pause or to a situation of monosyllabicity comes when suddenly an object of common interest is found and appears between the two dialogue partners. This is nicely described by Hans Citron[9] with regard to a chance conversation he overheard in a bus between a woman student and an apparently newly gained acquaintance. The dialogue began, "How long have you been in B?" There followed the answer and then a long pause. "What are you studying?" Answer; pause. And so it continued for a time. Suddenly and totally without expectation, the young girl asked her partner, "Do you like cats?" and this sentence rose between the two like a red balloon. Both looked at the balloon and met each other. After this strange test question the dialogue became easier, more lively, and actually had its real beginning.

Frequently, we also experience the opposite of a standstill in the flow of communications; we experience an extraordinary increase in the intensity of communication, so that our partner finally comes across to us as a monologizing endurance talker.[10] This person often belongs to the schizoid or hysterical type of character. Here a veritable flood of ideas is frequently combined with a certain stubbornness of thought completion. The monologizing endurance talker is always the proclaimer of a half-truth that he has picked up from the message of someone more prominent and which he, under the provocation of a desired martyrdom, passes on with exaggerated pathos. Jung named this type of person the "disciple archetype."[11] Faced with such a person, it is a matter of our not allowing the desired martyrdom to become reality but rather of letting the stream of talk flow over us in extreme objectivity, even if it seems insignificant to us, and of searching for significant data.

(*c*) Changes in the content of communication, which suddenly bring questions in response to questions, diversionary maneuvers, changing the subject, extreme politeness and compliance, vague statements, stereotyped repetitions, or even aggressive utterances, indicate with particular clarity that a state of emotional tension has now been entered. At first we will look for key words to reinsert into the dialogue, but by changing the subject we will be able to give relief whenever we have the impression that our partner is falling into too strong an emotional tension—in the process, however, always remembering that we absolutely must learn the causes of this strong emotional tension and blockage at some time during the dialogue.[12]

BREAKING OFF THE DIALOGUE

A dialogue can be broken off because the client leaves on his own, or because he asks that the dialogue be permitted to end, or because the pastor sees the impossibility of further dialogue. It can also happen, however, that a pause stretches out so long that the pastor is seized by panic and takes what the Catholic pastoral psychologist Walter de Bont calls a shot into the blue:[13] he throws out onto the table just any idea whatever, which then, as a rule, is also incapable of leading the dialogue further and bringing it forward. We would like briefly to summarize the most important reasons for breaking off a dialogue and give a few examples in each case. They are taken in part from Walter de Bont's little book *Faustregeln für das Seelsorgegespräch* (Rules of thumb for pastoral dialogue).

1. If the pastor does not adjust to his role as the client's dialogue partner and has a defeatist attitude, the dialogue will necessarily move toward termination. De Bont gives the following example, in which the client is a young, engaged soldier of rather loose character. The scene is the pastor's office.

> *Client:* I live now in P. I'm bored to death there. But I just came back from Holland. Six weeks ago. There I got my hands on a pile of money. Foreign pay supplement. And as a noncommissioned officer, I get quite respectable pay. Now, last Sunday I was with a whore again in Hamburg. That happens from time to time. Simply because I have too much money. I can't hold on to it. And when I got the girl in my car, I almost wanted to give her a twenty-mark bill and say to her, "Now, beat it!"
>
> *Pastor:* Yes, but these are things that you yourself must decide one way or the other. Of course, I can tell you that you ought not to do it, but what good will that do you?

De Bont comments,

> This priest takes up his position as a pastor, to be sure, but he is a pastor who has nothing to offer. The client himself holds the view that he should not do this, but he knows no process by which he can achieve this end. Indeed, he comes to the pastor precisely because he hopes that the latter is more knowledgeable. Yet before the client has presented his problem, the pastor is already of the opinion that he is not equal to this problem.[14]

2. Also, an incorrect question technique must be mentioned again in connection with the termination of dialogue. An example of this is the following skeleton of a dialogue in which only the questions of the pastor are presented: "How's it going? How long have you been lying in the hospital? A long time, then? Did you count on that? How long has it been now? Is your wife at home? How does it look with your disability pension? Pause. Did your son, as I've heard, do well on the test? And so forth until the final breaking off of the dialogue."[15] In counseling that consists so exclusively of questions—and, of course, questions that, in regard to interrogatory technique, must be labeled unsuitable questions—two factors again and again become acute: (1) the client feels that he is undergoing a cross-examination and mobilizes all his defensive powers against it, or (2) the question game gives the impression that the pastor will solve the problem as soon as he has gathered together all the pieces of the jigsaw puzzle, and so the client falls into complete passivity. Both lead without fail to the fruitless termination of dialogue.

3. A dialogue can also be broken off because a common basis of communication cannot be achieved. An example is the following dialogue, which has, to be sure, a pronounced pastoral and even theological character; yet the pastor presents only arguments from his own world of ideas, which is completely different from the client's ways of thinking.

> *Client:* If God wants to reign, then he shouldn't have made human beings free, so that they could do evil; then he could have reigned.
>
> *Pastor:* Then they would also lose their attraction. They would just be machines then. If your children do something good because

you have drilled it into them, can you then still admire your children? No, for then the children no longer do it out of conviction, but because you demand it. You can't be happy about that either. You can be happy only when it happens spontaneously, without compulsion. For then the children do it on their own. A machine is still admired, but only because it functions so well. You'll never feel an attraction for it.

Client: I find all of that very difficult.

Pastor: And what do you think about Christ? He had to deal with the same problem.

Client: I don't know. People say that he is the Son of God, that he is God. But I don't know that.

Pastor: I don't know that either. But I believe it, and isn't it remarkable that God allows his own Son also to suffer? I mean, that his suffering is as big a problem as our suffering. When we have resolved his suffering, then our suffering will also be resolved.

Client: Who knows?

With this, the dialogue had reached a dead end.[16] The pastor held completely firm, and this necessarily led to breaking off.

4. There is also the possibility that a dialogue will continue outwardly but inwardly has already been broken off, in that the outward understanding is, of course, maintained but one can sense no inner connections at all between the two participants' contributions to the discussion. Here, from hospital pastoral care, is a dialogue with a terminally ill woman patient over seventy years old:[17]

Pastor: I am the Protestant chaplain and would like to visit with you. How are you? I can see it's very hard for you.

Patient: Just as the Lord wills, Chaplain. But these young nurses! You'll pray for them too, won't you? They're so insolent.

Pastor: Oh, they're still young! Do you have any major complaints?

Patient: You know, it's because of my illness. Sometimes I can no longer hold my bowel movement. It's so terrible when it goes into the bed. I call, of course, but they don't come right away. Sometimes I think the Lord has rejected me.

Pastor: You may be certain that God has accepted you with all that you are. In the hospital we learn painfully sometimes that we are not only spirit, but also body, that we can't always do what we want. God loves you even in your suffering. I want to tell you that very definitely. The nurse told me that you've had a birthday.

Patient: Yes, I had a birthday yesterday, but . . .

Pastor: On birthdays at home we have sometimes read the 103d Psalm. May I read a few verses of it aloud?

Patient (after the psalm has been read): Yes, that's beautiful. I thank you, but . . .

Pastor: On a birthday, one also looks back. Wouldn't you like to tell me how things have gone in your life?

Patient: I grew up in M. After my schooling I went for a time into another household. But then I was called home, because my mother was sick. I nursed her several years, until she died. Then I took care of my father a long time, until he also got sick and died. But . . . Well, then I went to my brother, who lived in S, and kept house for him. When he died too, I came to my sister, who had a job, and cared for her until she died. And then I was all alone and had gotten old. So I went into an old folks' home, but . . .

Pastor (deeply moved): So, your whole life has always been a life for others. That's the way it was, earlier, with the daughters of a family. At least with the older ones.

Patient: Yes, earlier it was different from today, but . . .

Pastor: Now, if you could have chosen as a girl whatever vocation you wanted to choose, what would you have chosen?

Patient: I would have become a teacher, but . . .

Pastor: Now you have grown old entirely in the service of others, and now you are sorely plagued by your illness. Think again about the psalm that I read to you. There it speaks of the service that God has done and still does for us frail and sinful human beings. Can you join in with the "Bless the Lord, O my soul"?

Patient: Thank you, pastor.

When a common basis for communication cannot be achieved, the cause can also lie in the fact that the one who comes to the pastor is not prepared for confrontation with the kind of counseling that we have tried to characterize as the nondirective method. For example, the Catholic pastoral psychologist Louis Monden[18] reports that even here cases have been observed where the client tries to break off the dialogue because, as he distinctly says, "I came here not to pursue psychology but to hear from you the Word of God." And here this reaction was elicited only through the attentive listening of the priest. According to Monden, however, it represents an attempt to flee in order to avoid a real encounter.

5. Misunderstanding in a dialogue must also be named as one of the reasons for its termination. An example is the following hospital visit. The patient was operated on, two days earlier, for the eleventh time. Now he is no longer in the same room as in previous weeks. He got a corner bed in another room, so that he can look out into the yard. When the pastor enters, he is lying on his side with his back turned to the visitor.

> *Pastor:* Ah, you have moved.
>
> *Patient:* I have to lie on my side. I can't turn over; otherwise I would do so.
>
> *Pastor:* Oh, just stay as you are. You don't need to worry about that. Well, how's it going? You've already been operated on again?
>
> *Patient:* I have a lot of pain. But today it's already better than yesterday. They operated the day before yesterday.
>
> *Pastor:* That must surely be the third time already, isn't it? *(He senses immediately that he has put his foot in his mouth. He should have known the answer from earlier visits.)*
>
> *Patient (showing no ill humor):* The eleventh time. I have eleven holes in my back. Three big ones and eight little ones. I have been operated on every week.
>
> *Pastor:* But if the pains have already gotten milder . . . then you can begin again to look up *(the patient's expression shows that he does not understand; the pastor thought the patient would not assume that he meant "up" to God)* . . . look up toward recovery; then things will go better for you again. *(The patient seems not to share this view, either with regard to the present pain or the good progress.)*
>
> *Patient:* I still have a lot of pain, even if it's a little better today than yesterday. *(Pause.)*
>
> *Pastor:* Here you have the good fortune of seeing spring arrive.

The pastor's mistake, according to the reaction of the patient, is not so much that he did not remember exactly how often this man had already had surgery as that he did not catch the nuance in the man's answer. He had less pain, to be sure, but it was still severe. Therefore the patient repeated his statement once again and then became silent. The pastor did not know how to use this silence other than through a shot into the blue (the arrival of spring).[19]

What possibilities are there, then, for dealing better with the termination of dialogue? I can give only three pointers: Under no circumstances may the breaking-off of a dialogue be taken as the final ending. It should be answered either with the offer of a continuation or with the offer of a clarification of the misunderstanding that has emerged. When the pastor considers his own possibilities totally exhausted, then the offer should be made, in any case, to call on some other source of help.

DEPENDENCIES

Just as forcible termination must be regarded as a critical point in counseling, we must also concern ourselves with its opposite, namely, when a dialogue comes to no structural end and we must presume that some sort of dependency relationship has developed. We feel that our partner cannot bring the dialogue to a close and in hectic activity repeatedly throws out new topics and perhaps, even after announcements that the end of the dialogue is now near, reacts with more new material. It can also happen that our partner conveys to us the feeling that he cannot seize the opportunity of the proffered freedom and makes no use of it. His contact is that of an anxious child, and he is careful to make our positions and opinions obligatory for himself. A third possibility, finally, is that we have the feeling that the dialogue has acquired an illusionary atmosphere that is more appropriate to the intimacy of a congenial or romantic relationship than to the objective give-and-take between client and counselor.

What motives can lie behind such a dependency relationship? First, a large role is surely played by the anxiety of being alone in our society. There are certainly more people than we normally assume for whom a visit to the pastor is born solely out of a motive that lies in their loneliness. Then they experience a conversation, and toward the end of the dialogue anxiety over loneliness hits them with particular force. Furthermore, the often-experienced weak ego and infantilism of our partner can, of course, also be responsible for the fact that we are dealing with a "clinging vine," with a person who can hardly turn loose. And finally, there can indeed also be the possibility of an instinctive bond, which can be of the aggressive as well as the heterosexual or homosexual kind.

What possibilities do we have for dealing better with such dependency relationships? First, one should always guard against taking one's partner to task over such a dependency relationship in an interpretive or even reproachful manner. The usefulness of such interpretation, actually, is hard to see, and the harm can be substantial. If we should be mistaken, we would often put ourselves in a very embarrassing position. It appears more reasonable, when we feel an especially strong attachment by our partner, to make at least an attempt to find the person a home in some kind of fellowship. At this point, we must keep fully in mind that the present structure of our congregational life is not conceivably suited for giving a home to somewhat difficult and spiritually unsettled people. This is the unanimous experience of the telephone crisis ministry. Thus we have no choice but to make an attempt to create special institutions for such people within the present Christian community. If we choose to overlook the motivation that seems to lead to the particular attachment of our client and believe ourselves capable of giving him help in maturation, then the somewhat strongly expressed readiness for relationship could be the occasion for offering a longer series of dialogues, which nevertheless must clearly limit the amount of attention and also must be restricted in regard to the time period of the extension. Perhaps in the most favorable position is the one who, in the situation of a growing dependency relationship, can make the offer of another counselor. In no case should this offer be allowed to give the impression of being pushed away; it is most easily made where the client is prepared from the beginning for the fact that he is coming not to an individual person but to a circle of colleagues who are ready to deal with the issues addressed here.[20] With that, we are already touching on the question of structural change in the present efforts in pastoral care, upon which we are to focus in the next section.

6. The Dialogue Series

THESIS: The dialogue series represents counseling that extends over a longer period of time. If possible, its purpose, its goals, and its duration should be clarified and determined beforehand. The first contact, the first session, and the form of continuing sessions are subject to certain basic methodological principles. As a special form of the dialogue series, care and support represent a ministry of neighborly presence wherever, in a situation of concrete need or conflict, there is—from the standpoint of human judgment—nothing more that can be done to help. The end of a dialogue series comes into view when the pressure of suffering is diminished, when greater adjustment has been achieved, or when other sources of help have been made accessible. It must be prepared for methodologically.

The carrying-out of a dialogue series presupposes in the sphere of pastoral care a different structure of congregational ministry from the one generally present. The structural changes thereby necessitated are already being sought by many in a direction that can be described briefly as follows: First, among colleagues a certain development of specialization takes place according to individual talents, interests, or the continuing education acquired. It is incomprehensible why someone who is decidedly reticent should absolutely have to be forced to carry on lengthy and ongoing pastoral counseling with another person, and why it should be possible for one who has acquired special knowledge in this area, and also feels a particular impetus in this direction, to be so obstructed by other duties that he never even gets to these tasks.

Second, the new style of pastoral implementation definitely includes the training of a working team. It should include, on the one hand, experts who command specific, detailed knowledge of the complexity of today's living conditions, and on the other, of course, lay people who can be schooled in carrying on pastoral counseling themselves. What has today, after only a few years, already become a matter of course in the working methods of the telephone crisis ministry, namely, that one confides not in an individual but in a working group, could also have validity for all other forms of pastoral endeavor for the people of today. Only then will it be assured that the first contact can succeed in a methodically directed and considered fashion and that the importance of details will be taken seriously: how appointment making is done, how much waiting time will be asked of the client, and how definite office hours can be maintained. In the context of a pastoral endeavor carried out through team effort, the first session will have the special function of deciding whether in this case it is a matter of a one-time dialogue that perhaps ends with a referral, whether short-term or long-term pastoral counseling is appropriate, or whether here one can initiate what we can term pastoral care and support. Just as important as the beginning of such long-lasting care and support is its conclusion. We must have an idea of when the conclusion of such a dialogue series seems indicated, how it is prepared for, how it is carried out, and what the client's resulting perspectives on the future are.

THE FIRST CONTACT

The first contact is often of decisive importance for a longer dialogue series. Above all, there is a fundamental difference depending on whether this first contact was initiated by the client or by the pastor. If the first contact comes from the client, then the following factors must be considered:

1. A very important question, which one must, in any case, also make conscious, is the reason for the contact, which of course shapes the initial understanding and expectations of the client. There are several possibilities: Either he comes on the personal recommendation of another individual, in which case

the experience of the other person will have already given a particular shape to the expectations of the one seeking counseling. Or he comes because of an impersonal recommendation through some sort of notice, announcement, or something similar. Then it will be important to learn the nature of this announcement of the possibility of carrying on such a dialogue. For counseling carried out under the auspices of the church, it will, moreover, be of some importance to ascertain the extent to which the client sees us as a representative of the church and whether he comes to us because of that or in spite of it. Or finally, there is the possibility that he comes to me as a person whom he has come to know through a personal contact or as the result of a public appearance in a lecture or a sermon. His ideas and expectations could possibly be based on certain characteristics in this role of a public appearance, which are perhaps not yet completely clear and conscious even to himself. It behooves us therefore even in an initial dialogue to raise at some point the question of the motive or reason for the dialogue and perhaps to seize upon it.

2. Another very important question is whether the threshold of contact can be maintained at a very low or at a very high level. As an extreme example we could mention the telephone crisis ministry, in which the threshold of contact is held extremely low. It requires almost no individual effort from the client and remains in a noncommittal state where the breaking of contact is possible at any moment in the dialogue. Or the threshold may be kept extremely high, as in psychotherapy, for example, which requires from the client a considerable amount of personal initiative, effort, and will, just to get it started. In between these two extremes, of course, will lie the amount of individual initiative that must be demanded in order to have a promising, longer series of pastoral dialogues. Past experience in the work of counseling has shown that for pastoral counseling that may be ongoing, it is decidedly disadvantageous for an appointment to be made through a third party. The result has been, namely, that very many clients do not keep the appointments that were made for them. In general it has proved more expedient to ask the

client to make his own telephone call, in which he can personally make an appointment. This call can be received either by the pastor himself or by an appropriate staff member. One should remain flexible in regard to the amount of information that the client must give in such an appointment-making call. There are people who are not even ready to give their name. Even this should be accepted, but an effort should be made, when making such an appointment, to obtain the name, the approximate age range, and if possible also an idea of the problem.

3. In the case of a pastoral-care team, there is the possibility, after making such an appointment, of selecting a partner for the client. In so doing, the following considerations can play a role: first, professional knowledge; then, other special areas and talents, and the age as well as the personal experience of the pastor or counselor.

4. Finally, some attention should also be given to preparation for such a dialogue. This means especially a little greater awareness in the pastor or counselor than we are generally accustomed to, an awareness of information I already have about the counselee who is coming to me, some conscious examination of my own reactions to this information, and if need be, a little awareness of the personal situation in which I find myself right now and of those factors that could possibly become impediments in the dialogue situation.

If the initiative comes from the pastor, we are faced with an incomparably more difficult situation. It is exemplified by the serious problems of the pastoral home visit. Winkler has pointed out the special problems of this situation in a small work on pastoral psychology.[1] In every pastoral visit that is not motivated by some clear reason, one must realize that the other person feels himself subjected to a strange activity, that he takes every request as a demand and reacts accordingly, that superficially he indeed behaves appropriately yet subliminally is painfully affected and therefore instinctively shuts himself off. The clearer the reason for a home visit, the more comprehensible will be the situation. Nonetheless, the raising of questions in such a dialogue will always be the pastor's responsibility, and special attention must be given in conducting the dialogue until it succeeds in actually bringing the client into the center of the discussion. The home visit, it seems to me, hardly provides the basis for a dialogue series of longer duration.

An especially bad starting point seems to be offered by a home visit that is instigated by a third party. If it is a private individual, we must reckon with gossip and emotions in the background; if, however, it is a matter of an official, an agency, or a court—for example, in connection with the reconciliation attempts related to divorce that are carried out in many jurisdictions—then from the very beginning we must reckon with a defensive reaction from the client. In such a case, it seems more promising to forgo a home visit and issue instead an invitation to come in for a talk. We will find this situation above all whenever one spouse comes to us and expresses the enthusiastic wish now to have the other one also "summoned" for counseling. Nevertheless, the character of an official subpoena is, in any case, to be avoided; even in a letter in which one invites someone for a talk, the lack of compulsion in such a pastoral offer must be clearly expressed. In most cases it is probably better, when possible, to use a telephone call to present the possibility of a more personal contact.

THE FIRST SESSION

In discussing the constellation of interpersonal dynamics in counseling, we have already determined that the atmosphere in which the dialogue takes place and the associations that are evoked by the outward context can be important. The counseling room should be as far removed from the germ-free sterility of a doctor's office as it is from the undisturbed neglect of a bohemian apartment. We should be very clear about the fact that the outward condition of the room in which we conduct counseling can say a lot about ourselves that we do not necessarily have to hide but which must come into play in the constellation of interpersonal dynamics. If possible, even the seating arrangement should leave a little free choice to the client or at least not convey the feeling of some kind of natural inferiority. This is easily and unintentionally possible when the counselee has to look into the light or feels himself to be sitting well below his partner.

The opening of a dialogue will begin, as a rule, with an introduction if the counselee is unknown, but then it needs some kind of introductory flourish or formula. This can perhaps be nonverbal if, for example, I simply signal my readiness for dialogue and wait quietly for the other person to begin. Only if this causes my partner difficulty will I decide upon an initial question. In any case, this question must be as open as possible. It should be neither detached nor insistent and should be appropriate to the style of the pastor, so that a formulaic foreign body does not create an atmosphere of unreality from the beginning. Under all circumstances, at the beginning of a dialogue one should avoid interrogation and note-taking on personal information. The question as to whether notes may be made during counseling is answered variously. If one feels that one cannot do the task without such notes, the agreement of the counselee must be obtained in any case. It seems better to me, at any rate, for such notations to be undertaken after the end of the session in the absence of the client.

One of the most important points for the constellation of the first dialogue is the first entrance of the pastor. In every case it must occur consciously and be consciously selected. It may consist of assistance with articulation, a question, or a summary and clarification.

Special care is required for the close of the first session. If necessary, its approaching end should be announced ten minutes ahead of time, for the first dialogue requires, in any case, a session summary that, above all, contains an outlook toward the future. At this point the decision must be made whether this single dialogue will suffice or whether it will be a question of making another appointment. This decision, in any case, should be left to the client. Once it is made, however, a definite appointment should be agreed upon. In the process, one should already have in mind what is to take place at this new session. Unfortunate, in any case, are vague prospects for a continuation of the dialogue some time or at the right opportunity.

After the first session it is absolutely essential to formulate a sort of evaluation and prognosis, that is, to ask oneself the following questions: What was in this first dialogue? Approximately what period of time will the anticipated dialogue series require? Whose help and what supplemental information do I need, and what can I undertake myself by way of preparation for this series of sessions? What does the client expect, and which of his expectations are realistic, fulfillable, or unfulfillable?

THE SECOND AND THIRD SESSIONS

The opening of the second session in a dialogue series is frequently difficult because the client is unsure as to what he can presuppose concerning his dialogue partner's recollections of the first session. Right when he has a desire to be taken seriously and to have been important and interesting to the pastor, he moves decisively toward the opposite extreme and assures us that with our great workload and the many people who come to us, we could hardly still remember what was discussed the last time. One can avoid this difficulty by posing an opening question that recalls what was discussed in the last hour, brings a personal interest to expression, and builds the client a bridge for crossing over immediately into a continuation of the dialogue.

In very many second and third sessions it will come about that the client's need to articulate is initially satisfied, that for the time being he has said all that he wanted to say, and that now a clarification of further sessions must be undertaken. Here a decision will have to be made regarding whether to go to a shorter dialogue series or whether to develop, over a longer period of time, extended counseling or even care and support.

Here we will summarize only the criteria of a briefer counseling series: It is indicated whenever it is only a matter, at least in the beginning, of an opportunity for the client's self-expression, when we can elicit a need for information in certain limited areas, or where we see a chance to satisfy this need for information. A series of dialogues stretching over a shorter time period also seems to be indicated where it is a question of helping the client to a clearer formulation aimed at a particular goal or where it is a matter of expanding understanding in a limited area. Frequently a few sessions can also contribute to the client's growth in self-confidence and to his visualizing possible courses of action that were previously closed for him. Also the examination (not the execution!) of behavioral modifications could be seen as the task of the shorter dialogue series.

COUNSELING VERSUS CARE AND SUPPORT

In general, a series of dialogues lasting over a longer period of time is called counseling. It should already have become abundantly clear that by this term we do not mean that such counseling consists of giving bits of advice; it represents, rather, the effort, with a regular amount of attention, to hold dialogues that have an inner connection and have their content focused on a particular goal. We would like to clarify the problems of pastoral counseling by means of four questions:

1. When does it seem indicated?
2. What does it offer?
3. How does it do that?
4. How may counseling be distinguished from care and support?

1. Counseling is always conflict counseling. Its prospect lies in the effort to make a conflict situation expressible, understandable, and thereby surmountable. What conflict situations can we differentiate from one another? First, there is the conflict within oneself. According to the conceptual model of psychoanalysis, it is designated the conflict between psychic authorities. The result of such a conflict situation is either a psychosis or a neurosis. As an area of responsibility in conflict resolution, these phenomena fall outside the realm of pastoral counseling. A conflict resolution in the case of an intrapsychic conflict will belong exclusively in the hands of an expert, and for this reason it cannot be seen as a task for pastoral counseling.

A person can, however, also get into other conflicts, for example, into a conflict with his destiny. Here the question of meaning immediately comes up. In the realm of pastoral counseling, it should not lead too quickly into the question of theodicy or the question of predestination. Here it seems reasonable to ask, first of all, the question to what extent a person himself is his own fate and unconsciously shapes his destiny. A great many of these fate conflicts offer a good opportunity, through an understanding of biographical details, to help the person to a deepened understanding of meaningfulness in his own life. Above all things, it is the conscious interaction with the two large groups of drives, libido and destrudo, that allows one to discover meaningful events where one previously saw only ominous fate. It seems to me that above all in regard to aggression there is a broad area for more conscious interaction with one's own future destiny.

Another conflict is what I call the conflict of roles, which includes the quest for social prestige and especially the roles of man and wife, parents and children, supervisors and employees. Here the problem of role expectations and role prejudices largely forms the raw material of conflict, which can be released on a more conscious level in counseling. Even in the conflict with other people, the greatest difficulty consists in the fact that such situations are so incomprehensible and thus so crippling. They appear, therefore, to form a broad area of opportunity for helping to make these conflicts comprehensible. Finally, we must point to the conflict with that which is of ultimate concern: to that area which those in the laity would like to address very exclusively as the "genuine" pastoral area.

2. In such situations, what can the dialogue series offer? It offers, first of all, practice in the possibility of verbalization and thereby a little more conscious interaction in such cases of conflict. It offers, further, an aid to understanding that can reach into three areas: first, an understanding of emotions and personal feelings that, by being experienced in the interpersonal situation of the dialogue in homeopathic doses, as it were, can be understood as models and thus can offer the key to other situations. It offers, second, the aforementioned understanding of a previously uncomprehended collection of biographical data, and finally, it offers an understanding of the situation. Yet if we want

to be a little more demanding, we can reclaim for pastoral counseling what one can designate as help in maturation. We will thereby be able to make advantageous use of the concepts of those organizing forces that bring about maturation in human life, and can therefore say that this help in maturation presupposes the establishment and maintenance of a secure relationship, that it offers the possibility of identifying with someone, and that this identification is to be dissolved again through a discussion in which one's own standpoint and one's own conviction are won. And finally help in maturation can be designated as the practicing of denial in regard to our instinctive impulses. The dialogue situation already offers the possibility of experiencing and understanding such denials of the experience of satisfaction and of using them as models for further experiences with other people.

3. The leading of the dialogue in such a dialogue series will not differ essentially from what we have already discussed in regard to conducting dialogues in general. Here we simply point to three key concepts that play a certain role with the longer time period: We must provide for a certain *continuity* by keeping in mind the main theme of the dialogue. We must *establish connections* that the one trying to verbalize his conflicts cannot see. And finally, we can come to a certain *broadening of horizons* by introducing new points of view.

4. It is recommended that one make a distinction between counseling, which always seeks to alleviate conflicts, and care and support, which are no longer concerned with affecting the conflict event itself but are limited to offering a person in very great difficulties a little neighborly presence. Among such great difficulties are psychotic illnesses, depression in its various forms, incurable diseases, and that great catch basin of personality deviations that one customarily designates as psychopathic.

There is a whole range of people suffering under a psychosis whom pastoral support—always carried out in cooperation with a psychiatrist—can spare the hard fate of being committed to an institution. Thus, the work of the Berlin telephone crisis ministry was able, over a long period of time, to care for a transit worker who had developed the delusion of having invented a perpetual-motion machine, who was ridiculed by all and finally felt himself threatened. In the process, the telephone ministry avoided trying to talk him out of his delusion as well as affirming him in it. But having the opportunity every two weeks to make contact with an understanding and concerned person was enough to make possible for him the orderly perception of his other life functions.

The care of depressed people could also become increasingly the special task of pastoral care if the pastor, together with an expert, has determined whether it is a question of a *reactive depression* that can be interpreted as the response to a recent experience of loss, a *neurotic depression* that consists in the failure to work through the problems of early childhood, or an *endogenous depression* that may have some pathological process in one's physical makeup as its primary cause. Whatever is done therapeutically for the depressed person, when another human being is present who makes no attempt to help him out of his depression but within it contributes, by being present, to his finding the meaning of his own problems, this will certainly be felt to be helpful and can contribute to protecting people from rash attempts at suicide.

Surely the most self-denial is required for the care of so-called psychopaths, who have difficulties with their surroundings everywhere and frequently are not very sparing with their aggression. Such cases will determine whether the pastor has achieved the personal maturity that will allow him to forgo the satisfaction of his own needs in pastoral care. They could therefore become the touchstone of whether the lessons that were supposed to be conveyed in this book as the prerequisite of competent pastoral care have been worked through not only cognitively but also emotionally.

Notes

INTRODUCTION

1. I have indicated the results of a first, small, private survey on the topic of pastoral care—which was made only under the protest of many pastors—in "Zur Lehre von der Seelsorge," *Theologia Practica* 2 (1969): 140ff.

2. I refer here especially to Heije Faber and Ebel van der Schoot, *Praktikum des seelsorgerlichen Gesprächs,* 3d ed. (Göttingen, 1971), as well as Dietrich Stollberg, *Therapeutische Seelsorge,* 2d ed. (Munich, 1971).

3. So aptly expressed by Hans-Dieter Bastian, "Vom Wort zu den Wörtern," *Evangelische Theologie* 28 (1968): 28.

4. Cf. Paul Tillich, *Systematic Theology,* 3 vols. (Chicago: Univ. of Chicago Press, 1951), 1:8.

5. Klaus Heinrich has recommended for designation as one such "question" of present-day humanity "the threat of being identical to nothing; the threat of being speechless in the face of the powers of destruction; the threat that anxiety over loss of identity and speechlessness will drive one to self-destruction" (*Parmenides und Jona* [Frankfurt am Main, 1966], 67).

1. PASTORAL CARE AND LANGUAGE

1. Joachim Bodamer, *Gesundheit in der technischen Welt* (Freiburg, 1967), 65–66.

2. Ibid., 57.

3. Hans Asmussen, *Die Seelsorge,* 3d ed. (Munich, 1937), 15.

4. Ibid., 15–20.

5. Eduard Thurneysen, *Die Lehre von der Seelsorge* (Munich, 1948), 93ff.

6. Ibid., 109.

7. Ibid., 110.

8. Ibid., 111.

9. Ibid., 123.

10. Hans Otto Wölber, *Das Gewissen der Kirche* (Göttingen, 1963), 184–85.

11. Thurneysen, *Die Lehre,* 114.

12. Asmussen, *Die Seelsorge,* 17.

13. Horst Fichtner, *Systematik der Seelsorge* (Leipzig, 1931), 64–65.
14. Adolf Allwohn, *Das heilende Wort* (Göttingen, 1958), 204.
15. Hans-Joachim Thilo, *Der ungespaltene Mensch* (Göttingen, 1957), 75. In his more recent publications Thilo has clearly distanced himself from this position, esp., e.g., in *Beratende Seelsorge* (Göttingen, 1971).
16. Ibid., 78.
17. Adelheid Rensch, *Das seelsorgerliche Gespräch*, 2d ed. (Göttingen, 1963), 13ff.
18. Ibid., 19.
19. Ibid., 27. One would do Rensch's book an injustice if one did not note that the book also accentuates throughout striving to draw the person toward independence and to set him free. But that striving is repeatedly compromised through tension with a "firm, goal-directed leadership," which stands in the foreground in the pastoral dialogue (see pp. 206–7).
20. Thilo, *Der ungespaltene Mensch*, 76.
21. Allwohn, *Das heilende Wort*, 208.
22. Wolfgang Böhme, *Beichtlehre für evangelische Christen* (Stuttgart, 1956); Max Lackmann, *Wie beichten wir?* (Gütersloh, 1948); Oskar Plank, *Evangelisches Beichtbüchlein* (Stuttgart, 1956); Walter Uhsadel, *Evangelische Beichte in Vergangenheit und Gegenwart* (Gütersloh, 1961); and Max Thurian, *Evangelische Beichte* (Munich, 1958).
23. David Riesman, *The Lonely Crowd* (New Haven: Yale Univ. Press, 1950), 6ff.
24. Alfred Lorenzer, *Sprachzerstörung und Rekonstruktion* (Frankfurt am Main, 1970), 152ff.
25. Thus Erich Fromm, *Psychoanalyse und Religion* (Konstanz, 1966), 99.
26. Thus Ronald D. Laing, *The Politics of Experience* (New York: Pantheon Books, 1967).
27. A crossing of these two themes is circumscribed by Johann Christoph Blumhardt with an attitude that he repeatedly adopted, with "Wait and hurry" as a familiar quotation (cf. Joachim Scharfenberg, *Johann Christoph Blumhardt und die kirchliche Seelsorge heute* [Göttingen, 1959], 105–6).
28. Sigmund Freud and Oskar Pfister, *Briefe* (Frankfurt am Main, 1963), 135–36.
29. Peter Homans, *Theology after Freud* (Indianapolis: Bobbs-Merrill, 1970), 85ff.
30. Otto Haendler, *Grundriss der Praktischen Theologie* (Berlin, 1957), 71, 369–70.
31. Klaus Heinrich, *Parmenides und Jona* (Frankfurt am Main, 1966), 27.

32. Wilhelm von Humboldt, "Über die Verschiedenheiten des menschlichen Sprachbaues," in *Werke* (Darmstadt, 1963–), 3:225.

33. Ibid., 428, 28, 195.

34. Ibid., 226, 20.

35. Ibid., 196, 429, 252, 139, 418.

36. Ibid., 421, 221, 228, 220.

37. Hermann Wein, *Sprachphilosophie der Gegenwart* (The Hague, 1963), 36.

38. Ludwig Wittgenstein, *Schriften* (Frankfurt am Main, 1963), 8.

39. *Tractatus,* sec. 1, 1.12, 2, 4.024.

40. Karl Otto Apel, "Wittgenstein und das Problem des hermeneutischen Verstehens," *Zeitschrift für Theologie und Kirche* 63 (1966): 51, 52, 61; with ref. to sec. 3.325, 4.112, 4.027.

41. Wittgenstein, *Tractatus,* sec. 5.631, 5.632.

42. Apel, "Wittgenstein," 57; cf. Wittgenstein, *Tractatus,* sec. 4.003.

43. Werner Heisenberg, *Physik und Philosophie* (Berlin, 1965), 61. Benjamin Lee Whorf makes the same point clear in regard to understanding time. "We say 'ten men' and also 'ten days.' . . . But 'ten days' cannot be objectively experienced. We experience only one day, today. . . . Our tongue makes no distinction between numbers counted on discrete entities and numbers that are simply 'counting itself' [as in the basic awareness of 'becoming later and later']. . . . This is objectification." (*Language, Thought, and Reality* [Cambridge: M. I. T. Press, 1956], 139–40).

44. Carl Friedrich von Weizsäcker, "Sprache als Information," in *Die Sprache,* ed. Emil Preetorius (Munich, 1959), 49.

45. Ibid., 53, 38.

46. Heisenberg, *Physik und Philosophie,* 38.

47. Johann Gustav Droysen, *Historik* (Munich and Berlin, 1937), 234, 225, 287.

48. Klaas Heeroma, *Der Mensch in seiner Sprache* (Witten, 1963), 75.

49. Heisenberg, *Physik und Philosophie,* 36–37, 85, 145, 150.

50. Wittgenstein, *Schriften,* 325–26 (*PI* 68, 71).

51. Ibid., 336, 338, 343, 479 (*PI* 89, 92, 111, 664).

52. Ibid., 342 (*PI* 109).

53. Ibid., 347 (*PI* 133).

54. Ibid., 393 (*PI* 255).

55. Ibid., 343 (*PI* 116).

56. Ibid., 300 (*PI* 23).

57. Apel, "Wittgenstein," 76.

58. Wittgenstein, *Schriften,* 389 (*PI* 241).

59. Ibid., 333 (*PI* 83).

60. Ibid., 381 (*PI* 199).

61. Ibid., 383 (*PI* 206).
62. Apel, "Wittgenstein," 79.
63. Georg-Friedrich Jünger, in *Die Sprache,* ed. Preetorius, 58, 61.
64. Whorf, *Language, Thought, and Reality,* 67–68.
65. Jean-Paul Sartre, *Das Sein und das Nichts* (Frankfurt am Main, 1951), 278.
66. Heeroma, *Der Mensch,* 110.
67. Wein, *Sprachphilosophie,* 36.
68. Ibid., 71, 151, 65.
69. Heeroma, *Der Mensch,* 110.
70. Ibid., 116.
71. Ibid., 118.
72. Dietrich Rössler, *Der "ganze" Mensch* (Göttingen, 1962), 50.
73. Ibid., 94–95.
74. Ibid., 96.
75. *Neue Zürcher Zeitung,* 17 December 1967, p. 6.
76. Cf. Johannes Hempel, *Heilung als Symbol und Wirklichkeit* (Göttingen, 1958), 287, 305.
77. Ibid., 311; and *Theologisches Wörterbuch zum Neuen Testament* 3:210.
78. Johann Christoph Blumhardt, *Die Krankheitsgeschichte der Gottliebin Dittus,* 6th ed. (Hamburg, 1950).
79. Friedrich Zündel, *Johann Christoph Blumhardt* (Zurich and Heilbronn, 1880), 107.
80. Ibid.
81. Ibid., 108.
82. Ibid., 113.
83. Ibid., 114.
84. Friedrich Seebass, *Johann Christoph Blumhardt* (Hamburg, 1949), 25.
85. Zündel, *Blumhardt,* 118.
86. Ibid., 123.
87. Ibid., 129, 130.
88. Freud and Pfister, *Briefe,* 126.
89. Sigmund Freud, *Gesammelte Werke,* 17 vols. (London, 1953–), 16:241.

2. BASIC FORMS OF DIALOGUE

1. Thus, e.g., Eberhard Müller: "The teaching dialogue is not a genuine dialogue" (*Die Kunst der Gesprächsführung* [Hamburg, 1954], 12).
2. Otto Friedrich Bollnow, *Sprache und Erziehung* (Stuttgart, 1966), 67.
3. Gerhard Ebeling, "Profanität und Geheimnis," *Zeitschrift für Theologie und Kirche* 65 (1968): 91.

4. Cf. Joachim Scharfenberg, "Verstehen und Verdrängung," *Theologia Practica* 2 (1968):130ff.
5. Bollnow, *Sprache und Erziehung,* 17.
6. Ibid., 70.
7. Ibid., 68.
8. Ibid., 69.
9. Erwin Metzke, "Die abendländische Kultur des Gesprächs und ihr Verfall," in *Medicus Viator,* ed. Paul Christian and Dietrich Rössler (Tübingen, 1959), 315.
10. Werner Jäger, *Paideia,* 2 vols., 2d/4th ed. (Berlin, 1959), 2:11.
11. Ibid., 22.
12. Müller, *Die Kunst,* 11.
13. Metzke, "Die abendländische Kultur," 317.
14. Ibid., 318.
15. Jäger, *Paideia* 2:117.
16. Ibid., 121–22.
17. Ibid., 105.
18. Metzke, "Die abendländische Kultur," 319.
19. Jäger, *Paideia* 2:145.
20. Ibid., 147.
21. Friedrich Nietzsche, *Über die Zukunft unserer Bildungsanstalten,* 5 lectures (Kröner ed., 1871–72), 5:496.
22. Ludwig Pongratz, "Das psychologische Explorationsgespräch," *Psychologische Rundschau* 8 (1957): 197.
23. Ulrich Moser, "Gesprächsführung und Interviewtechnik," *Psychologische Rundschau* 15 (1964): 263.
24. Peter R. Hofstätter, "Die soziale Dynamik der psychotherapeutischen Beziehung," *Psyche* 10 (1957): 733–34.
25. Pongratz, "Das psychologische Explorationsgespräch," 197.
26. Moser, "Gesprächsführung und Interviewtechnik," 264.
27. Pongratz, "Das psychologische Explorationsgespräch," 199.
28. Moser, "Gesprächsführung und Interviewtechnik," 265.
29. Ibid.
30. Pongratz, "Das psychologische Explorationsgespräch," 200.
31. Thus Hans Jürgen Eysenck, *Wege und Abwege der Psychologie* (Hamburg, 1956), 6.
32. Ruth Bang, *Hilfe zur Selbsthilfe* (Munich and Basel, 1960), 19.
33. Ibid., 34.
34. Cited by Maria Kamphuis, *Die persönliche Hilfe in der Sozialarbeit* (Stuttgart, 1968), 32.
35. Ibid., 66.
36. Ibid., 79.
37. Bang, *Hilfe zur Selbsthilfe,* 21.
38. Ibid., 39.

39. Ibid., 22.
40. Cf. ibid., 80ff.
41. Ibid., 150.
42. Ibid., 125–26.
43. Thus ibid., 151–52.
44. Kamphuis, *Die persönliche Hilfe,* 37.
45. Ibid., 38.
46. Ibid., 67.
47. Hermann von Waldegg, "Das seelsorgerliche Gespräch," *Pastoralblätter* 105 (1965): 547.
48. Hans-Heinrich Knipping, "Verkündigung als Gespräch," *Pastoraltheologie* 55 (1966): 35.
49. Martin Ohly, "Verkündigung und Gespräch," in *Phantasie für Gott,* 3d ed., ed. Gerhard Schnath (Stuttgart and Berlin, 1970), 77.
50. Metzke, "Die abendländische Kultur," 320–21.
51. Ernst Lange, *Chancen des Alltags* (Stuttgart and Gelnhausen, 1965), 125.
52. Dietrich von Oppen, *Frömmigkeit in einer weltlichen Welt* (Stuttgart and Berlin, 1959), 30ff.
53. Ohly, "Verkündigung und Gespräch," 71.
54. Ibid., 74.
55. Müller, *Die Kunst,* 14.
56. Ibid., 27.
57. Hans Jürgen Schultz, *Kritik an der Kirche* (Stuttgart and Freiburg, 1958), 150.
58. Ohly, "Verkündigung und Gespräch," 76.

3. **INTERPERSONAL DYNAMICS IN DIALOGUE**

1. For what follows, cf. Joachim Scharfenberg, "Übertragung und Gegenübertragung in der Seelsorge," in *Forschung und Erfahrung im Dienste der Seelsorge,* ed. E. Kiesow and Joachim Scharfenberg (Göttingen, 1961), 80ff.
2. Sigmund Freud, *Gesammelte Werke,* 17 vols. (London, 1953–), 1:97.
3. Ibid., 147.
4. Cf. Sigmund Freud and Oskar Pfister, *Briefe* (Frankfurt am Main, 1963), 406.
5. Freud, *Gesammelte Werke* 1:167–68.
6. Ibid., 310.
7. Ibid. 14:305.
8. Ibid. 5:281.
9. Ibid. 8:55.
10. Ibid., 374.
11. Ibid., 364.
12. Ibid. 14:305.

13. Ibid. 10:135.
14. Carl Gustav Jung, *Psychologie der Übertragung* (Zurich, 1946), 11.
15. Gerhart Scheunert, "Psychoanalytische Situation und zwischenmenschliche Beziehung," *Wege zum Menschen* 10 (1958): 40–41.
16. Carl Gustav Jung, *Von den Wurzeln des Bewusstseins* (Zurich, 1954), 67.
17. Fritz Riemann, "Bedeutung und Handhabung der Gegenübertragung," *Zeitschrift für psychosomatische Medizin* 7 (1960): 123–24.
18. Freud, *Gesammelte Werke* 8:108.
19. Jung, *Psychologie der Übertragung*, 23.
20. Ibid., 38.
21. Ibid., 127.
22. Ibid., 25.
23. Frieda Fromm-Reichmann, *Intensive Psychotherapie* (Stuttgart, 1959); Karen Horney, "The Problem of the Negative Therapeutic Reaction," *Psychoanalytic Quarterly* 5 (1936): 29–44; and idem, *Neurosis and Human Growth* (New York: W. W. Norton & Co., 1951), 201ff.
24. Franz Heigl, "Die Gegenübertragungsangst und ihre Bedeutung," *Zeitschrift für psychosomatische Medizin* 6 (1959): 32.
25. Jung, *Psychologie der Übertragung*, 22.

4. **MEANS AND METHODS IN COUNSELING**

1. Ulrich Moser, "Gesprächsführung und Interviewtechnik," *Psychologische Rundschau* 15 (1964): 271.
2. Ruth Bang, *Hilfe zur Selbsthilfe* (Munich and Basel, 1960), 110ff.
3. Moser, "Gesprächsführung und Interviewtechnik," 274.
4. The transcription of this dialogue was graciously provided by the pastoral counseling work group of Pastor Lutz, of Stuttgart.
5. Moser, "Gesprächsführung und Interviewtechnik," 271.
6. In addition to the articles of Moser and Ludwig Pongratz, the latter cited in n. 22 of chap. 2, I draw, in the following, on Stephen A. Richardson, Barbara Snell Dohrenwend, and David Klein, *Interviewing: Its Forms and Functions* (New York: Basic Books, 1965); W. V. D. Bingham and B. V. Moore, *How to Interview* (New York: Harper & Bros., 1959); and Ernst Kretschmer, *Medicinische Psychologie* (Leipzig, 1941).
7. William Shakespeare, *Hamlet*, act 2, scene 1.
8. Richard Meili, *Lehrbuch der psychologischen Diagnostik* (Bern, 1955), 166ff.
9. Cf. Maria Kamphuis, *Die persönliche Hilfe in der Sozialarbeit* (Stuttgart, 1968), 80.
10. Cf. Richardson, Dohrenwend, and Klein, *Interviewing*, 198.
11. Hans Jürgen Eysenck, *Behavior Therapy and the Neurosis* (New York: Pergamon Press, 1964), and Liane Blöschl, *Grundlagen und Methoden der Verhaltenstherapie* (Bern, 1970).

12. Rudolf Cohen, "Grundlagen der Verhaltenstherapie," *Wege zum Menschen* 23 (1971): 460.

13. Ibid., 462.

14. The individual procedures are described in detail in Blöschl, *Grundlagen und Methoden.*

15. Peter Gottwald, *Verhaltenstherapie: Grundlagen, Ergebnisse, aktuelle Aufgaben* (Hamburg, 1971), 44.

16. Cohen, "Grundlagen," 470.

17. Cf. Gottwald, *Verhaltenstherapie,* 48.

18. Cohen, "Grundlagen," 463.

19. Gottwald, *Verhaltenstherapie,* 48.

20. Carl R. Rogers, *Client-centered Therapy* (Boston: Houghton Mifflin, 1951).

21. Rainer Bastine, "Einführung in die klienten-zentrierte Gesprächstherapie," *Wege zum Menschen* 23 (1971): 481.

22. Ibid., 482.

23. Heije Faber and Ebel van der Schoot, *Praktikum des seelsorgerlichen Gesprächs,* 3d ed. (Göttingen, 1971), esp. 191ff.

24. Klaus Winkler, "Tiefenpsychologisch orientierte Beratung," *Wege zum Menschen* 23 (1971): 450.

25. Cf. pp. 12–13 above.

26. Cf. the close of the case presentation in Winkler, "Tiefenpsychologisch orientierte Beratung," 459.

27. I would therefore also like to register my doubts about the mixing of self-exploration and interpretation as proposed recently by Hans-Joachim Thilo (see his *Beratende Seelsorge* [Göttingen, 1971], 93).

5. **CRITICAL POINTS IN COUNSELING**

1. For the following, cf. Joachim Scharfenberg, "Das Problem der Angst im Grenzgebiet von Theologie und Psychologie," *Wege zum Menschen* 20 (1968): 314ff.

2. Anna Freud, *Das Ich und die Abwehrmechanismen* (London, 1952).

3. Cf. Gustav Bally, "Ärztliche Behandlung als dialogische Leidenshilfe," *Wege zum Menschen* 9 (1957): 209ff.

4. Cf. Kurt Lewin, *Die Lösung sozialer Konflikte* (Bad Nauheim, 1953), 128–29.

5. Hermann Nunberg, *Allgemeine Neurosenlehre* (Bern and Stuttgart, 1959), 281ff.

6. Ulrich Moser, "Gesprächsführung und Interviewtechnik," *Psychologische Rundschau* 15 (1964): 263ff.

7. Harald Schultz-Hencke, *Lehrbuch der analytischen Psychotherapie* (Stuttgart, 1951), 214ff.

8. Stephen A. Richardson, Barbara Snell Dohrenwend, and David

Klein, *Interviewing: Its Forms and Functions* (New York: Basic Books, 1965), 204.

9. Hans Citron, "Über das Gespräch," *Wege zum Menschen* 16 (1964): 420.

10. Otto Jäger, "Erziehung zum Gespräch," *Wege zum Menschen* 16 (1964): 231.

11. Carl Gustav Jung, *Die Beziehung zwischen dem Ich und dem Unbewussten* (Zurich, 1951), 36.

12. Cf. Moser, "Gesprächsführung und Interviewtechnik," 227.

13. Walter de Bont, *Faustregeln für das Seelsorgegespräch* (Freiburg/Basel/Vienna, 1968), 65.

14. Ibid., 16–17.

15. Ibid., 29–30.

16. Ibid., 30–31.

17. Graciously provided by the pastoral-counseling work group of Pastor Lutz, of Stuttgart.

18. Louis Monden, *Sünde, Freiheit und Gewissen* (Salzburg, 1968), 128.

19. De Bont, *Faustregeln,* 63–64.

20. Cf. Joachim Scharfenberg, "Telefonseelsorge und ihre Verbündeten," *Wege zum Menschen* 15 (1963): 31ff.

6. **THE DIALOGUE SERIES**

1. Klaus Winkler, "Pastoralpsychologische Aspekte des Gemeindebesuches," *Wege zum Menschen* 15 (1963): 201ff. Cf. also the treatment of the theme "Der seelsorgerliche Hausbesuch," in *Lebendige Seelsorge* 1 (1965), and Marie Simmon-Kaiser, *Besuch und Begegnung* (Freiburg, 1968).

Index